Fugitive from Spanish Fascism

A Memoir by Miguel Domínguez Soler

Fugitive from Spanish Fascism

A Memoir by Miguel Domínguez Soler

Translated and with an Introduction by Richard Barker

Cornerstone Press
University of Wisconsin-Stevens Point

© 2009 by Richard Barker

All Rights Reserved. Published 2010

Originally published as *Ayamonte, 1936: Diario de un fugitivo, Miguel Domín-guez Soler,* Francisco Espinosa Maestre and Manuel Ruiz Romero, eds.

© Huelva: Diputación, 2000

Translated and printed with permission of

La Diputación de Huelva.

Printed in the United States of America

Library of Congress Control Number: 2009938326

ISBN: 978-0-9774802-8-9

Pictures on the cover:

Typical Spanish handwriting of the 1930s. Credit: Richard Barker

German Chancellor Adolf Hitler (not shown) and Spain's Generalissimo
 Franco salute together, in Hendaye, France, Oct. 23, 1940, during Hitler's
 trip to France, Spain and Italy. Credit: Associated Press

Typical Spanish portico. Credit: Leah Wierzba

Cornerstone Press

University of Wisconsin-Stevens Point

Stevens Point, WI

www.uwsp.edu/cornerstone

Maps by Corinna Neeb

Geographic Information Systems Center

University of Wisconsin-Stevens Point

Contents

Translator's Introduction — i
About the Translation — x

Fugitive from Spanish Fascism

July 18, 1936	3
First News	14
Uncertainty	19
In Town	22
The Killings Continue	32
Deceit	37
Exposed	40
What General Yagüe Said	43
A New Hiding Place	46
The Humiliating Parade	50
The Executions	52
The Leader of the Coup Pays Us a Visit	54
Flight	55
The First Letter	73
An Honest Trade	77
Days Go By	81
The Incident	84
En Route to Lisbon	87
The New Family	91
I Pay My Friend a Visit	95
More News	98
Journalistic Lies	100
In Cintra	103
The Meeting in Cintra	106

Departure	109
En Route to Casablanca	115
Poor Da Rosa	122
The European War	126
In Bouarfa, Desert Capital	138
Into the Desert	142
Rassemblement	147
Work	149
Inauguration of the First Stretch of the Trans-Saharan	156
An Official Threat	160
Departure	164
At the Police Station	168
The Housewarming Party	172
The Arrival of the Mayor of Ayamonte	176
I Become Productive Again	182
The Landing of the Americans	184
My American Guests	193
The Meeting with the Americans	199
The Boat	203
In Agadir	206
The Little Moorish Girl	214
Production	217
Cada Oveja con su Pareja	220
Casablanca	223
The Factory	226
Homecoming	227

Reference Materials

About the Translator	228
Maps	232

Translator's Introduction

During historical research, the most interesting discoveries are occasionally made while looking for something else. Miguel Domínguez Soler's Memoir is just such a case. In early 1997, Manuel Ruiz Romero was preparing his senior thesis in Contemporary Spanish History. The subject he had chosen was the first pre-autonomic government of the Junta of Andalusia.[1] Among the documents he uncovered was a typewritten letter from a Spanish expatriate named Miguel Domínguez Soler to Rafael Escuredo, the second pre-autonomic president of the Junta. It was sent from Safi, Morocco, and was dated February 11, 1980, shortly before a referendum concerning access to autonomy for the Andalusian region. The writer wished to vote yes on the referendum. The letter includes many autobiographical details:

> *Dear fellow Socialist: With my sincerest greetings for your prominence in our organization, and in keeping with what is said of you in the newspaper "The Socialist," <u>I can do no less</u> than congratulate you.*

[1] Manuel Ruiz Romero, *Política y Administración Pública en el primer Gobierno Preautonómico de Andalucía. La gestión de Plácido Fernández Viagas al frente del ente preautonómico* (Seville: Instituto Andaluz para la Administración Pública, 2000).

I am an Andalusian, always an Andalusian, from the town of Ayamonte in the province of Huelva, and the last remaining disciple of Don Blas Infante Pérez, who was martyred for his ideas. I joined the Party in 1930 thanks to the activities of my teacher Don Blas, who was more a Socialist than anyone else. He carried out his work unpretentiously, teaching us the difference between separatism and autonomy. That was long ago. . . .

The purpose of this letter is to send you my affirmative vote regarding Andalusian autonomy. The elections have been arranged hastily. The government, or lack thereof, should have made known in the press and radio that Andalusians living abroad should present a sealed envelope with their vote, yes or no, in the consulates nearest their place of residence, giving their names and surnames and their birthplace. In that way, thousands of votes could have been gathered, because there are thousands of us Andalusians living abroad. The consuls could have sent those envelopes the next day to the Junta of Andalusia so they could be counted. But it is too late now.

I am 70 years old and have spent the past 42 years in exile. I have tried to get my fellow Socialists, the delegate Carlos Navarrete, or the mayor of Huelva, J.M. Marín Rite, to find a solution to my problem as a former employee of the Huelva provincial government, expelled from my post and condemned to death in 1936. I continue living with the hope that my remains will not end up in some Moroccan cemetery.

I ask nothing of you.

I send my affirmative vote for the autonomy of my beloved region.

I embrace you and wish you success. You are young and take our place in the struggle.
Signed:
Miguel Domínguez Soler
P.S.: If you wish, I will send you ample information on Don Blas, and what he went through when his first daughter was born in Isla Cristina, where the upper classes triumphed against him because he did not want to baptize her. "He was a democrat and for that reason he yielded. Because we are democrats still...."[2]

The letter, written little more than four years after the death of the Spanish dictator Generalissimo Francisco Franco, offers a tantalizing glimpse into the life of a man who led an eventful life. He was born in Ayamonte, in southwest Spain, located near the Atlantic coast just across the River Guadiana from Portugal, and he grew up during the reign of King Alphonse XIII. At the age of twenty, he joined the Spanish Socialist Party one year before the proclamation of the Second Republic, Spain's ill-fated democracy. In 1936, he was an employee of the Huelva provincial government when Generals Franco, Mola, Queipo de Llano, and others, backed by the upper classes, the Catholic church, and the Falange, Spain's Fascist Party, rose up against the legally constituted government, elected by universal suffrage. Like so many others at the time, Miguel Domínguez was purged from his profession and condemned to death for his political affiliation. He somehow managed to escape and, at the age of seventy, was living in exile in Morocco. Despite his age, and all he must have suffered for his beliefs, he had not lost his democratic and socialist ideals. He hoped to

---

[2] The typewritten letter sent to the Andalusian president from Safi, Morocco, is in the Andalusian General Archive, dossier 470.

return to his beloved Spain and was acutely interested in the political changes taking place in his country in the wake of Francisco Franco's forty years in power. He also displayed a critical attitude toward "the government, or lack thereof," that was steering Spain back to democracy.

The information in the letter about Miguel Domínguez's life had little bearing on the topic of Manuel Ruiz's senior thesis on Andalusian autonomy. What most intrigued the young researcher were the references to Blas Infante Pérez. During the Monarchy and the Republic, Blas Infante had been a tireless proponent of Andalusian autonomy and had published his ideas in the national press and in numerous books, beginning with *Ideal andaluz*.[3] For a while he had lived sixteen kilometers to the east of Ayamonte in the town of Isla Cristina, where he supported himself as a notary public. Manuel Ruiz Romero was well-acquainted with the bibliography regarding this man, who was assassinated by Fascists on August 10, 1936, and who, in 1983, would be named "The Father of the Andalusian Homeland" by the Junta of Andalusia. Personal contact with a man who described himself as "the last remaining disciple of Don Blas Infante Pérez" could confirm or revise the current historiography concerning what was called "Historical Andalusianism."

When Manuel Ruiz discovered Miguel Domínguez's letter in 1997, seventeen years had passed since it was written, and the letter's author would be eighty-seven years old. Consulting long distance information, the young researcher was able to find Miguel Domínguez's phone number in Safi, Morocco, and contact his wife, who informed him that her husband had died several years before.

---

3 Blas Infante Pérez, *Ideal andaluz* (Seville: Imprenta de J. L. Arévalo, 1915).

The widow had acquired Spanish citizenship through marriage, spoke Spanish, and had taken the name María del Carmen, but she was Moroccan by birth. Her Arabic name was Abouch Mohaiti Gaugui. She provided Manuel Ruiz with some biographical information concerning her late husband: for instance, that his post with the Huelva provincial government during the Republic was that of scribe at the Ayamonte Hospice. In fact, she was planning to travel to Ayamonte to make arrangements to receive a widow's pension. Manuel told her how he had become aware of her husband and why he had been interested in contacting him. She was unable to provide information about her husband's relationship with Blas Infante, but she expressed interest in the preservation of her husband's memory in his native land and spoke of the existence of many papers, poetry, correspondence, and other unpublished writings she had saved as a vivid reminder of her self-taught husband's intellectual and literary pursuits.

In September 1997, when Abouch Mohaiti was in Ayamonte arranging to receive a widow's pension, Manuel Ruiz went to meet her and spent several hours with her, during which time she showed him a sample of her husband's unpublished poetry and the letters he had saved. Seeing Manuel's disappointment that the material was of little historical interest, she announced the existence of a typewritten manuscript in which her husband related the story of his life. Although Manuel was skeptical, the Moroccan widow insisted he read the manuscript and, if he thought it worthy, do what he could to have it published so her husband's life would not be forgotten. She agreed to send the manuscript from Morocco to a mutual friend in Ayamonte, who would pass it on to Manuel.

In March 1998, Manuel received a letter from Abouch Mohaiti informing him that the manuscript was in the hands of their mutual friend in Ayamonte. Manuel went again to the town where this friend told him of the importance of Miguel Domínguez's autobiography, the clarity of the writing, and the accuracy of his descriptions of the violent days in Ayamonte at the outbreak of the civil war, descriptions that coincided with the stories that had been handed down from generation to generation about the Fascist repression. In fact, some of these stories included references to Don Miguel himself, who had become almost legendary for his remarkable escape from death at the hands of the Fascists. Manuel found the book to be truly extraordinary. It read like a novel of adventure, filled with suspenseful episodes. There was even a love story—in fact, three love stories. And the narrative ends with an unexpected twist. Indeed, the book could have been a poignant historical novel, were it not for the sad fact that the events were real.

Manuel had the manuscript transcribed as a computer document and sought the collaboration of the historian Francisco Espinosa Maestre, a specialist in the Spanish civil war, whose pioneering work on the Fascist repression in the province of Huelva had been published two years before.[4] Francisco Espinosa also appreciated the literary qualities of the Memoir, with the added value that Miguel Domínguez's account of the Fascist repression in the town of Ayamonte corroborated his own research and presented the events from the perspective of an eyewitness. In the preparation of his book *La guerra civil en Huelva*, Fran-

---

4 Francisco Espinosa Maestre, *La guerra civil en Huelva* (Huelva: Diputación, 1996).

cisco Espinosa had examined the municipal archives and interviewed residents in all the seventy-eight towns of the province of Huelva, compiling lists of those assassinated during the repression in each town. Only three of the seventy-eight towns in the province were spared the massacres carried out by Fascists, which caused a minimum of five thousand five hundred victims in the province. By contrast, in the days preceding the towns' occupations by the forces of the insurgent generals, violent confrontations between supporters of the military coup and defenders of the Republic had led to a maximum of one hundred forty-five victims among the former, and were limited to only fifteen of the province's towns.

For Ayamonte, Francisco Espinosa was able to compile a nominal list of ninety-nine victims of the Fascist repression as opposed to zero victims among the supporters of the coup. In the Spanish edition of the Memoir, published in 2000, Francisco Espinosa contributed several footnotes concerning the events and people who appear in the work.[5] The conclusion was clear. Miguel Domínguez's account of the repression in Ayamonte was absolutely reliable and would be a valuable addition to the many recent works on the suppressed history of the atrocities committed by the Right during the civil war that brought Franco to power.

We can also trust Miguel Domínguez's account of his life on the lam in Fascist Portugal where, if caught by the dictator Salazar's police, he would have been returned to Spain and shot. In mid-April 1939, he escaped to Casablanca, Morocco. The Spanish civil war had just ended

---

5 Francisco Espinosa Maestre and Manuel Ruiz Romero, eds., *Ayamonte, 1936: Diario de un fugitivo, Miguel Domínguez Soler* (Huelva: Diputación, 2000).

and the Second World War was only months away. With the same enterprise, charisma, and remarkable luck that enabled him to survive his life as a fugitive, first in Spain and then in Portugal, Miguel Domínguez joined the community of Spanish Republican refugees in the Moroccan capital and began to put his life back together, working in the sardine-packing industry. But then another disaster overtook him. With the Nazi occupation of France and General Pétain's armistice, a German Commission arrived to take charge of French Morocco. The consequences in Casablanca are depicted by Miguel Domínguez with a brutal realism barely hinted at in Humphrey Bogart's classic film. Spanish and other refugees from European Fascism were rounded up by the French gendarmes at the service of the Vichy government and handed over to the Germans. Miguel Domínguez became a slave laborer building the Trans-Saharan railroad. To make matters worse, he was again living under the threat of being sent back to Franco's Spain where he would have faced certain death by firing squad.

He was rescued from this living hell by his former employer and benefactor in Casablanca, Monsieur Mallein, who "rented" him to manage a sardine cannery in Safi, Morocco. Although technically still a "slave," he was owned by a friend and his life improved significantly. Then, on the night of November 8, 1942, Miguel left his sleeping quarters at the cannery to see why his dog was barking and encountered a group of American commandoes who had come ashore to scout out the enemy defenses on the eve of the amphibious landing in North Africa. As chance would have it, they were all of Hispanic origin—from Texas or Puerto Rico—and spoke Spanish. He was overjoyed when he asked what they were doing there and one of them replied, "We have come to liberate the peoples of Europe from Fascism." In one of many humorous anecdotes that appear throughout the Memoir, a commando from Texas, whose rudimentary knowledge of geography was sufficient for him to know he was in Africa, asked, "Are there lions around here?" To which Miguel replied, "*Hombre*, in the Casablanca Zoo there is a pair of them, but they are very old by now."

A free man again, our hero pursued a successful career in the fish-processing industry in Morocco while following with great interest the progress of the Allies in their battles against European Fascism. As the Second World War drew to a close, this enthusiasm turned to bitter disappointment as he and his fellow exiles in Morocco realized that the Western democracies had no intention of liberating Spain from its Fascist leader. In fact, by the 1950s, the United States would support Franco in exchange for the Spanish dictator's cooperation in the Cold War against the Soviet Union.

Throughout Miguel Domínguez's long life of tribulations, he was sustained by his optimism, his sense of humor, and his ideals. And by something else as well. In the course of his narrative he refers frequently to his "Diary." He found comfort and a sense of mission in his writing. Following his many brushes with death, he expressed the belief that he had been saved for a purpose: to bear witness to the cruel injustices of the twentieth century and the indomitable spirit of individuals who struggle to live in freedom. Like Melville's Ishmael, he survived to deliver a cautionary tale about fanaticism.

About the Translation

Translating Miguel Domínguez Soler's Memoir has been a real pleasure, but it has also presented numerous challenges. The author describes himself as an "intellectual worker." Miguel Domínguez was a graduate of "the great university of the common man," as he calls it. It was a vibrant "university" that was destroyed by the Franco regime. Its classrooms were the streets and cafés of Spain, and its libraries were in the meeting halls of Republicans, Socialists, and Anarchists. The author's prose reflects this education. He is capable of employing a surprisingly erudite vocabulary, sometimes influenced by the many foreign languages he acquired, but he is just as likely to write in the colloquial language of a Spanish worker. I have attempted to reproduce the different linguistic registers used in his writing without resorting to English clichés.

The most problematic decisions I had to make while translating the Memoir were presented by what an editor or writing teacher would call tense confusion. Miguel Domínguez alternates between the "historical present" and a more distanced style employing verbs in the past tense. These shifts sometimes occur in mid-sentence. In many instances, this stylistic peculiarity may be because the Memoir is the revised and edited version of a diary, now lost, that was possibly written in present tense.[6] But there may be another explanation. Miguel Domínguez's experiences were traumatic, and he seems incapable of remembering them without reliving the emotions that accompanied them. When the author switches to the historical present, the reader has the impression of witnessing the events as if they were unfolding before his or her eyes. I have encountered the same alternation between present tense and past tense narration while recording interviews for an oral history of an Andalusian town.[7] For the residents of Castilleja del Campo, just as for Miguel Domínguez, many of the events of their traumatic past would always be present. I have "corrected" Miguel Domínguez's "tense confusion" for only a few especially jarring cases. For the most part I have left it alone, out of respect for the author and because I believe it makes his account more vivid.

Finally, there is the matter of nicknames. Almost everyone in Spain and Portugal has a nickname. In most cases I have translated them. Thus, the Fascist thug 'El Trueno' becomes 'The Thunderclap,' and 'O Papa,' the Portuguese smuggler who teaches Miguel Domínguez how to go undetected in the countryside on the Spanish-Portuguese border, becomes 'The Pope.' In Spanish and Portuguese, the definite article is often an integral part of the nickname, so I have retained them in the translation. In a few cases, the nicknames, such as 'Rinquiño' or 'Misiño,' are untranslatable. I have left them in the original language.

---

[6] This is the opinion expressed by Francisco Espinosa Maestre in his introduction to the Spanish edition of the Memoir. Francisco Espinosa Maestre and Manuel Ruiz Romero, eds., *Ayamonte, 1936: Diario de un fugitivo, Miguel Domínguez Soler* (Huelva: Diputación, 2000), 40.

[7] Richard Barker, *El largo trauma de un pueblo andaluz: República, represión, guerra, posguerra*, (Castilleja del Campo: Ayuntamiento, 2007).

Fugitive from Spanish Fascism

July 18, 1936

I was born on March 1, 1910, under the sign of Pisces, in a town on the left bank of the mouth of the River Guadiana. Since I was the son of a family of workers, I had no other option but to join the class to which my mother and father belonged, because everyone was defined by the group into which he or she was born. For that reason, by the age of eighteen, I was already involved in the politics of the Spanish Left.

Then came that bitter day, July 18, 1936. It was after midday. A group of us citizens was sitting in a café in the town's center, just across from the old Republican Casino, founded the previous century. The mayor of the town, Don Manuel Flores Rodríguez, appeared and said to us, "I need forty willing men. I will arm them to maintain order and protect the border with Portugal. General Queipo de Llano, together with other troublemakers, has initiated a military rebellion in Seville against the legally constituted government. The Civil Guard from here is going to Huelva by order of the governor to join other Civil Guard units, and from there is going to Seville to crush the rebellion." The situation did not look good at all. We were perplexed.

"The governor shouldn't concentrate the Civil Guard units. He should have them arrested," I said.

The mayor's declaration spread throughout the town and, instead of forty, there were hundreds of citizens who wanted to cooperate in its defense, since the most immediate danger would come from Portugal, ruled by the dictator Oliveira Salazar. I was in a hammock when, at dawn on July 30, I was roused from my sleep and, rubbing my eyes which had rested only a few hours, my ears were abuzz with the news: the authorities that had governed the town and the province until a few hours before, together with my closest friends, had fled from the advancing Fascists in a workboat from the Port at eleven o'clock the night before and, according to what I was told, were on their way to Tangiers. At any moment, the first troops sent by the rebel generals would be entering the town. A mere "military coup" was turning into a civil war that was spreading with incalculable consequences. A few fugitives who had arrived in the town had already told us that the advancing forces had been rounding up and shooting people in the conquered towns. We doubted these terrible deeds, but the fact is they were being discussed.

I made a quick assessment of my situation: to the north and east of the town, the advance troops were approaching; to the west was Portugal, with a regime that opposed the Spanish Republic, and in which there was a fifth column of Spanish military men who had refused to accept, much less swear allegiance to, the Republic. These military men, with numerous supporters, were already gathering at the border and preparing to cross into Spain. The only possible escape route was to the south, in other words, the Atlantic Ocean, and to cross that sea we would have to acquire boats capable of reaching North Africa. I was already advised that the customs guards were under orders to stop all attempts to escape.

I was told that the schoolteacher, Don Manuel Chacón Díaz,[8] along with Salvador Feu and other friends of mine, were preparing to embark as well in another of the Port's workboats. When they were threatened at gunpoint by the customs guards, they had to abandon all hope of salvation by that escape route. All resistance was impossible. To resist would have meant sacrificing several young men with no training in the art of war, young men who had nothing more than shotguns loaded with birdshot with which to confront the machine guns that Hitler, the great demagogue and powerful ruler of Nazi Germany, had sent through Portugal.

"Why waste time with further vacillations?" I told myself. I put together a package with food and a few packets of tobacco and, smiling to conceal my bitterness, I left home for the countryside. It was in this small white town of southwestern Andalusia where there would unfold the cruelest drama that history had ever known.

Once outside the town, I climbed a small hill where there was an ancient castle and looked at my watch: it was five o'clock in the morning. From there, one could see how the town sloped down to the river. I turned to say good-by, believing that I would return in a few days to participate in the retaking of the town. The sun reddened the sky. It promised to be a hot summer day and there wasn't even the hint of a breeze. All day I walked under that scorching sun,

[8] For Chacón Díaz, see Francisco Espinosa Maestre, *La guerra civil en Huelva*, 457; for the declaration he was forced to make in the presence of the Falangists, Joaquín Gutiérrez Blanco and Alfonso Martín Navarro, on the day of his assassination, see the newspaper *Odiel*, August 19, 1936.

crossing streams and gullies. Every once in a while, I would see a shepherd tending his flock, happy in his ignorance. The sun was about to set when I arrived at a thick reed bed. "A good spot," I thought, "there is probably water there. I will rest and eat a little bread and cheese."

Suddenly, ten meters from the reed bed, a man emerged. I instantly thrust my hand into my unbuttoned shirt and drew my pistol. It was my guardian angel and my only defense in such situations. The stranger smiled at me. I got up and approached him. Soon I could see who he was: a well-known Portuguese smuggler who was emerging from his hiding place. He was known as 'The Pope.' He called to me by name and, removing his hat, wiped away his sweat. Then he invited me to climb up into the hills with him. What a fright he had given me! He told me that to remain by the stream was madness... Ah!, these crafty foxes who know every inch of the steep places where their nocturnal trafficking takes place, their advice is priceless.

Further uphill, we stopped in the darkness among some cliffs. He took a bottle of wine from his knapsack and offered me a few swallows. We ate bread and cheese as well as dried and salted fish that he gave me. Then he advised me not to return to the town because a great number of military men who, as I already knew, had gone into exile during the Republic, were there on the border. He had passed them the previous night. They were well-armed and had gathered by the pier under the command of a retired military officer named Pulido, who had been a physical education instructor for the boys of the town. For months, they had prepared for this offensive which they were about to carry out from Portuguese territory. Several barges, loaded with munitions, were awaiting orders to cross the River Guadiana.

"I give you my instructions," he told me. "First, do not approach places where there is a well, because there they (he was referring to the customs guards) are waiting in ambush to hunt you down. Second, you should spend the daylight hours in the lowlands, hidden in the vegetation, or among the cliffs. Never attempt to travel over hills during the day, because a person walking or standing on the heights can be seen from far away. Third, at night or when it is dark, one must take the highest route you can find along the way, because from the heights it is easier to detect danger and defend yourself or beat a retreat down the opposite side from where the enemy is approaching."

After several minutes of genuine camaraderie, he invited me to follow him. About five hundred meters further east, we were among some cliffs and he told me, "Here I guarantee that you will sleep undisturbed. Before the sun comes up, go back down to the stream." A quarter of an hour later, 'The Pope's' silhouette passed in the semi-darkness carrying a bulging sack. I supposed it was full of coffee, since at that time it was the most profitable contraband.

I couldn't sleep that first night of my life as a fugitive. A multitude of problems kept me awake. To continue walking that night was to risk falling off a cliff into a ravine or tangling myself in hawthorns. I waited for daybreak, but the approaching dawn caused me considerable anguish. I wished it to be dark forever because I believed the darkness protected me. My flight was so full of uncertainty, so insane, so lacking in direction.

As the new day broke, I was on the move. Following the instructions of the smuggler, I have headed downhill and begin traveling along the edge of the stream. After an hour of walking, when the sky was an explosion of gold and wonder, I make out a farmhouse. There was a field with bundles of wheat ready for threshing. "A good place to sleep for a few hours," I thought. Under cover of the reed bed, I began approaching cautiously. From there, I couldn't be seen; I, on the other hand, could observe everything from my hiding place. Then I saw someone heading up to the threshing floor. Suddenly, others began to emerge from the hay: first one, then two, then, little by little, up to twenty people. Some were armed with shotguns. They gathered together to talk. They did not look like military men. I began to move closer and closer, from thicket to thicket and, at last, I could see that it was a group of my best friends who, just like me, had escaped along the many trails that crisscross these hills and valleys, trails used by smugglers and customs guards. This was their meeting place. They greeted me and were amazed at my solitary escape. There was Eliseo Garlito, Don Manuel Chacón, Salvador Feu, Jesús Feria, Antonio Susino, Perfecto Alonso, Joaquín Guzmán. We had among us enough money to buy a few liters of milk at the farmhouse, and soon we were making loaves of barley bread, which allowed us to savor a much-needed breakfast.

We talk. No one proposes a solution to our bitter dilemma. There are two ways to escape: the first is to get to the sea and rob a boat that could take us to Tangiers, impossible without a struggle because the coast is being watched; the other is to keep crossing the mountains to the north and join the miners from the Río Tinto Copper Company, but from here to Río Tinto there are seventy kilometers of enemy territory to traverse. I have advised that we abandon this place as quickly as possible. The misfortune of many is a fool's consolation, as the saying goes. Whether true or not, what is certain is that, together, we felt stronger. Someone proposed that we head for Río Tinto where the miners were holding out. Others emphasized the distance to be traveled and that such a large group passing through enemy territory would lead to inevitable clashes with hostile patrols, making such an enterprise impossible. Almost everyone advocated seeking a hideout in the mountains, far from the river, to wait until the nation's government reestablished order. We would help. Others raised their voices in protest: "But we haven't killed or wounded or robbed anyone. Why are we so afraid? Why would they do anything to us? Some of us will go to jail because we are against Fascism and eventually they'll let us go. They aren't going to imprison the two-thirds of Spain that thinks like us."

Everyone gave their opinion. I kept mine to myself until we took a rest in the shade of some wild olive trees to escape the suffocating heat. I said to them, "I don't have any confidence in that band of criminals who want to bring down the government and grab power, and are ready to wipe out everyone who does not think as they do. You have already heard how they are shooting people wherever they go. It is the revenge of the rich who can't abide being governed by the people. Just look at 'The Thunderclap,' who is like a panther on the loose, and others who, like him, have probably crossed the border from Portugal. You can all do as you like. I am going to hold out as long as I can. Turn myself over to them? Never. If they come looking for me, I will defend myself to the last bullet. I have two cartridge clips in reserve. I will save the last bullet for myself in case there is no other way out."

We are on the move again. We have taken a useless detour and arrived at a high reed bed. I have told them about my encounter with the smuggler and have asked them to follow the instructions he gave me. I have begged them not to light matches that could reveal our presence. Some of them have rebuked me, saying, "How fearful you are!" Maybe it is fear, but I am cautious and here, now, one can't be too careful.

At the beginning of the third day, I found myself out in the open, away from the thickets and with the assignment of looking out for Joaquín Guzmán's signals. He was located on a mountaintop wearing a wide straw sombrero and with a dark blanket wrapped about his shoulders. It was the attire used by shepherds in that area. Joaquín Guzmán was a butcher by trade, a business he ran for himself. He used to buy livestock from the inhabitants of these regions and, for that reason, they gave him whatever he asked for.

From below, I kept an eye on our lookout while I shaved next to a pool in the stream, a kit with my toilet articles by my side, when Joaquín signaled to me. I scrambled up the bank by the stream, crouching as low as I could. Joaquín was signaling that two customs guards were approaching along the stream's edge preceded by a large dog of the breed we used to call a wolf-mix. I quickly dropped back down to relay the news to the rest of the group. Each of them readied their firearm and took cover as best they could behind the rocks.

Minutes later, the customs guards arrived. The dog didn't bark or dare to attack anyone. He was satisfied just to approach and sniff me, since I was the one who was exposed. The border guards greeted us with, "Good afternoon friends." They looked about and saw several fugitives. "We beg your pardon but we are here on a mission. We were looking for some nine millimeter Astra pistols that our lieutenant lent your mayor for the defense of the town. We ask whichever of you has those arms to return them to us because our superior has to answer to those people."

One by one, those who were hiding came forth and showed them the arms they had, which were not of the model they were looking for. They sat down on the rocks with our group and we chatted amiably. They advised us to return to the town. They said that the military men only arrested those who had blood on their hands. They knew that none of us had committed crimes or made attempts on anyone's life, so they added, "If any of you want to cross the river and take refuge in Portugal, we ourselves would help you." I have not intervened in the conversation but I felt like telling them that the other side of the Guadiana was seething with Portuguese guards who were under orders to arrest anyone who tried to set foot on Portuguese soil. The conversation with the border guards lasted almost an hour. They never even realized that Joaquín was one of us. Finally, they continued on down the same route through the reed bed, always preceded by the large dog they had with them.

At midday, the country estate called "Casa de la Viña" sent us a large wooden platter and a basket with tomatoes, onions, green peppers, a little salt, and two horns: one with oil and another with vinegar. Accompanying this succulent feast, there were two large loaves of barley bread. It was a gift from Joaquín Guzmán.

During the meal, I have advised them we should relocate, since farmers, shepherds, and, even worse, the customs guards knew where we were, which could cause us to be surrounded and marched through the town in handcuffs like common thieves. Some answered me sarcastically,

"How fearful you are." In response to the reproach, I have kept my silence. I will no longer give any advice. I will keep my fear to myself.

As evening came upon us I told them, "I am going to sleep on the highest point of that ridge. Whoever wants to follow me is welcome." My attire consisted of a white shirt, ashen-colored pants, and some canvas shoes with rubber soles. I also had my sack of provisions, my tobacco pouch, and my toilet articles. Up on the ridge, surrounded by high cliffs, there was total darkness and absolute silence. If I fell asleep, the approach of any person would wake me up. While thinking and thinking, I gradually closed my eyes and fell asleep. I was awakened by the sound of an animal that, only a meter away and startled by my presence, took off in panicked flight. I suppose it was a hare. I heard the barking of distant dogs, the croaking of frogs in the pools of the stream, the footsteps of someone on the pebbles in the ravine below. Eventually, I fell back to sleep.

At daybreak, I have opened my eyes. Every bone in my body aches from the hardness of the ground, but I feel in good health. Following the advice of that unforgettable smuggler, I descended from the heights down to the stream. I put my sack on the ground and took out a little tin box and extracted a bar of soap. I tried to lather myself but to no avail, because the resin from the pinweeds had soaked through my shirt. Then I followed the path through the reeds to the encampment. To my great surprise, I found only four people: Perfecto Alonso, Antonio Susino, Jesús Feria, and Joaquín Guzmán, who was already getting ready to take up his lookout post. The rest of the team, taking advantage of the night's darkness, had taken off to seek refuge in. . . the town. "The town?" I cried.

"And what else can we do?" said the others. "Life here is becoming impossible. Those who have gone back will look for influential people to vouch for them so as not to be arrested and will make arrangements to go on living."

Sure enough, Joaquín Guzmán climbed the hill, as he had done the day before. He donned his large sombrero and wrapped his blanket around his shoulders. He gave a whistle, raised his arms, and signaled. A little later, a Portuguese shepherd approached him and they exchanged some words. It took the shepherd a half hour to return with a bottle full of coffee and milk and a few pieces of bread. Joaquín came down and we all savored that succulent breakfast, taking a swig and passing the bottle around, since we lacked glasses. After breakfast, we talked and decided to wait until the next day. If we have not received favorable news, we will approach the town, and there each one can choose the course they think best.

The lookout was back at his post. It was nearly midday when he signaled that someone was coming toward us along the stream. We have found hiding places. Soon, from among the reeds, we recognize him. It was Manolito Beas, a boy about fourteen years old, the cousin of my fiancée, who was bringing us a packet of provisions wrapped in a towel.

First News

Manolito, the emissary, brought not only provisions, a little tobacco and matches, but, above all, fresh news from the town. We anxiously took in word by word the events that had occurred during our absence. The Fascists had entered the town on foot along the grading that had been laid for the projected rail line. They did not encounter the least resistance. One group was composed of Falangists from Seville and Huelva. Another very numerous group, that had come from Portugal, consisted of retired military men opposed to the Republic, and Portuguese elements recruited in that country, the beginning of what would become the "Viriato" group, in memory of the celebrated shepherd from the forests of the Sierra de Estrella who had led the inhabitants of western Iberia in an uprising against the Romans. They were well-armed. As I have pointed out, the military rebellion had been hatched in Portugal, from which we were separated by the River Guadiana, and which was ruled by the dictator Oliveira Salazar, an enemy of the Spanish Republic.

It was July 29, 1936, the day of the occupation. They organized a public demonstration which marched through the deserted streets of the town to the cry of "Long live Spain." They pounded on the doors with their rifle butts, forcing everyone inside to come out of their houses. For the most part, they found terrified women and children. Many people had fled the town and headed for a higher elevation called "La Recife" to wait things out, believing the "flood" would subside. Local Fascists immediately set about denouncing those they considered to be "reds" and the provocations, aggressions, and arrests began. By the evening of that first day, the jail was so full that on the following day they proceeded to place iron bars on the windows of the Creoli Cinema, which they also filled with anyone they considered to be enemies, such as those who had a membership card in the socialist General Workers' Union or in some political party and, above all, those they thought to be Freemasons. According to them, the Masonic lodges contained the democratic elite, and democracy was dead. They, the Fascists, had come to bury it.

While our young emissary spoke, I listened and pondered the situation. I remember, and it is worth remembering, that a few days before, General Queipo de Llano began the uprising in Seville with the affirmation that he was an impeccable Republican, and that he had launched the uprising to impose order in the country so disgracefully governed by pro-democracy politicians and wracked by the constant strikes carried out by the labor unions. The general ended his harangue with the cry of "Long live the Republic," after which the national hymn of the Republic was played.

The town's Fascists, along with outsiders, searched the houses of workers for arms and membership cards. They arrested vast numbers of people and, with great hypocrisy, consoled each of them by saying that nothing would happen to them since not a single drop of blood had been shed in the town. The more gullible of these workers and Republicans turned themselves in without the least resistance. Some were more cautious and hid in cisterns or closets. Everyone was suspicious.

As to me, the emissary said that an official letter had been brought to my house from the provincial government informing me that I was expelled from my employment "because I was considered an enemy of the National Movement," which I considered an honor because, in fact, I could not tolerate that military coup and would fight alongside all who thought as I did to crush it. The emissary's account continues, "At all moments of the day and night, to the accompaniment of drum rolls and bugle calls, one of the town's Falangists would read in a loud voice, as if he were the town crier, the orders of the military authorities." One of the strangest, from the previous night, was, "The town is invited to the train station to inaugurate the new rail line and the first arrival of the Huelva Ayamonte train. What the political parties did not achieve in sixty years, the Falange has done in two days."

"Imbeciles," I said, "now that they have found everything already finished."

Another of the orders was that all the gold in the possession of the town's and the surrounding area's inhabitants should be taken to the city hall. They have also begun beating and physically abusing all those considered enemies, and Manolito added that my fiancée went to see the Mother Superior of the Provincial Hospice, asking her, in view of my behavior toward the nuns, to intercede with the Falangists in case I was arrested, to spare me from mistreatment. That lady's reply was, "There is nothing I can do for your fiancé. It is the military authorities who now give the orders and make the decisions."

I keep thinking that we who support democracy are fools because our actions are based on good intentions and love of humanity. As she left the visitor's room, my fiancée was taken aside by one of the nuns most fervently devoted to the National Movement, who told her, "Do not fear for your fiancé, ma'am, we are very grateful to him. He, and he alone, saved the miraculous image of the Christ, and Christ will protect him as long as he lives." My house had been searched twice a day. Sometimes they had come at two in the morning and they had even stuck their bayonets through the mattresses of all the beds in case I was hiding in one of them. I realize what my situation is and am unshaken in my conviction that we are up against savages, and later, I called them "beasts on the prowl."

We bombarded our generous courier with questions. He has warned us not to attempt to cross the Portuguese border. The customs guards will look the other way and let us go by and then signal to the Portuguese guards that we are coming. As a result, all who pass are arrested and turned over, handcuffed, to the Spanish Falangists. The people who escaped from the border towns into Portugal have already been "expelled" in this way and, once returned to Ayamonte, it is said they are taken to the capital city, Huelva. That direction means execution and burial in the forests on the outskirts of town. They never got to Huelva. In just a few days, the sixty kilometers to Huelva have become well-known for the cries of pain and the sound of rifles being discharged. There had been scores of indiscreet witnesses who brought the news back to the town. They have begun arresting the mothers, wives, or brothers of those who have fled in order to convince them to turn themselves in. All the young men of military age had been mobilized and sent to recruitment centers.

At that moment, and when the conversation was the most interesting, three Portuguese airplanes passed overhead with the mission of locating and reporting the presence of groups of fugitives. It was to protect our enemies' backs. They have already installed J. Agua as mayor, and during his term in office, all the bad things that would happen transpired. It was about three in the afternoon and the way back to town was long, so I asked young Manolito to return to town before night fell and also asked him to bring me newspapers on his next visit. I warned him to take all necessary precautions to avoid being followed by the enemy the next time he came to see us.

Uncertainty

Far from all roads, our backs protected by cliffs, and with the thick curtain of reeds of the stream Arroyo Grande, and thickets, three of us resisters have remained: Jesús Feria, Antonio Susino, and me. As time passes, impatience gnaws away on our nerves. We need to know everything going on in the town, and that is difficult. I have won over the sympathy of the old Señora Isabel, owner of the country estate called "Casa de la Viña," who sent me provisions every day. The relatives of this lady made daily trips to town to sell their cows' milk, and brought me back details of what was occurring there. They warned me that 'The Thunderclap' and a certain 'Little Asparagus,' together with other criminals, traveling on horseback and armed to the teeth, were making the rounds of the area's estates, hunting down fugitives. Unlucky peasants from Sanlúcar, Castillejos, El Almendro, San Silvestre, and Villablanca had already fallen into their hands.

Of the three of us, I am the only smoker. It is a great effort for me to resist lighting indiscreet matches at night. We always spoke in a low voice. We positioned ourselves between the pinweed and cliffs in the highest part of the hill, and kept our ears alert to any noise coming from the direction of the stream. That is how we spent our hours on the first days of this hot August. We asked ourselves why we had been forced to flee. It seemed ridiculous that, without having committed any crime or misdemeanor of *lese humanité*, we were forced into hiding like vermin.

One night, my two friends propose to me that we return to town. We should approach at nightfall before the moon comes out, enter the town, and, separately, seek out a hiding place until governmental troops arrive to restore order. Our hope lay with the miners from Río Tinto, who, according to the milk sellers, had armor-plated trucks and cars, and were constantly attacking Moratilla's troops, that captain of the Huelva Civil Guard who, under the pretext of going to confront Queipo de Llano in Seville, had instead joined him and ambushed the column of miners who also went to Seville, ordering the execution by firing squad of the nearly one hundred and fifty miners who survived the trap.[9]

Against my wishes and full of distrust and fear, one night, crossing mountains and valleys, we arrived at a place called "Cuatro Caminos." There we parted company once and for all. I would see Jesús Feria again in Kenitra, Morocco, where he came to work in the tuna industry in

---

9 Although he must be referring to Lieutenant Morillo, attributing to him the responsibility for the ambush in La Pañoleta on the morning of July 19, we know that the true author and beneficiary of the operation was the Civil Guard commander Gregorio Haro Lumbreras, designated civil and military governor of the province of Huelva a few days later. Such a meteoric rise in his career was possible thanks to the physical elimination of the Civil Guard lieutenant Julio Orts Flor, loyal to the Republic and assassinated during the first days of August, following one of the first parodies of a court-martial carried out by the military insurgents.

1942. I need not say what that meeting was like. Jesús could not hold back his tears as we embraced. He showed me the scars he had on his back, the result of wounds received in jail, wounds from which were extracted pieces of his shirt that had become embedded in his flesh. He asked me how I had managed to escape and reach Morocco. I related to him the whole odyssey from "July 18, 1936."

I am on the outskirts of the town. I went to a sanatorium called "El Parral." My brother Pepe was there, convalescing from a heart lesion. That night, Pepe was in anguish, and even more so upon seeing me. He said, "Hide. They are looking for you everywhere. They have come with huge flashlights that blinded our eyes, rummaging everywhere." I tried to calm my brother. I know that later he died in the Huelva Hospital, far from my love and affection.

In Town

Once night fell, I entered Chanoca's bakery through the back door. Everyone was startled to see me. Chanoca has two sons, José and Ángel, held in the jail. I went up to the room above the oven, but I became distressed when I noticed that the windows had iron bars that made all hope of escape impossible in case of danger. I pointed it out to Chanoca, who understood my problem. He went out in the middle of the night and brought back a hacksaw, I don't know from where. I immediately began to saw away the bars. Once I had finished the job, I asked for a glass of saltwater to oxidize the shiny stubs of the bars so no one would suspect the cuts were recent. The oven was right under this room. That is where Serafín worked. He was of Portuguese origin, but had been raised all his life in Spain. From this room, now free of bars, I took advantage of the opportunity to jump to the adjacent rooftop terraces for training. To the right, was Juana Orta's terrace; in front, was the house that belonged to Carmen Soler, better known as 'The Canner'; and further down, was Martina Álvarez's terrace. In case of trouble, I am weighing the pros and cons for my defense.

I have complete trust in these people because, in addition to the fact that Chanoca was related to my mother, he and his whole family have always expressed socialist ideas. They explain to me how, on the day the Falangist hordes entered the town, these hordes stormed a bicycle shop in La Laguna, next to 'El Gato's' wine shop, robbing everything that was there. They did the same to all the stores and residences belonging to those they considered enemies of the Movement.

A few meters across the way is my fiancée's house, and her family has already been apprised of my presence. I hear the bugle calls and the orders that no one is to go out at night without authorization from the military authorities. Well-armed Falangist patrols go by, singing the Falangist hymn, and with constant shouts of "Long live Spain." Sometimes they raise their arms in the Roman *Ave César* manner, just like when the gladiators used to fight in the Coliseum.

I have only slept a few hours during the night. At dawn, I am up and alert. Serafín went out and, a half hour later, returned in a state of alarm. At once, I hear wailing and shouts from up the street. A great tragedy had begun. Chanoca and Serafín come up to see me. They are pale. I can imagine what had happened. "They have killed someone," I said. Serafín fills in the details: at dawn, at the intersection with the highway to Villablanca, among the pine groves, twenty-four bodies have been found. Twenty-one of them were men and three were women, all natives of the town. They had been left there on display to paralyze all human will or rebelliousness by instilling terror in the populace. Several of the town's "rich kids," among them 'Rinquiño,' went there in an automobile to see the bodies and laughed when they saw the awkward positions of the cadavers: Martina Álvarez; Adelina 'The Pastry Maker'; Carmen Soler 'The Canner'; Manuel Álvarez López; the blacksmith, Manuel Picón; Castelo 'The Gimp'; José Naranjo; Manolo Franco 'Beret' (better known by their nicknames than by their given names); and finally to the list was added Joaquín Guzmán, the butcher, who had been our friend.[10] At that moment, his sister, Juanilla Guzmán, was coming up the street shouting as if insane, "Murderers, murderers!" It broke my heart.

Serafín had not slept. He had spent the night in front of the oven, but at dawn, I begged him to go into the casino to listen to the conversations of the wealthy young men and tell me what they were saying. By now, whatever sensitivity a person might possess is lost. One comes to feel what an irrational beast lurks within, and one's heart turns hard. The event has been a warning for me to be prepared and to defend myself in case of danger. And Chanoca has two sons in the jail, José and Ángel. They are there with hundreds of defenseless citizens who have committed neither murder nor theft.

By now I have learned the details of the first bloodletting. It was midnight when the truck arrived at the door

---

10 Among the different people mentioned by Miguel Domínguez Soler as victims of the repression at various points in his narration, Manuel Franco, Arturo Pessoa, Ángel Espinosa, and a certain Casillas were never entered in any Civil Death Registry. All the others do appear, but with dates of death different from those indicated in Miguel Domínguez Soler's diary. The dates in the Civil Death Registry can be seen in Francisco Espinosa Maestre's, *La guerra civil en Huelva*, 564-6. The entry of incorrect dates of death in the Civil Death Registry, which can be seen in numerous cases throughout the province of Huelva, demonstrates the desire for obfuscation with which the inscriptions were carried out. Not only were the inscriptions made outside the legal time limit, but with erroneous dates. And we are speaking here only of those "privileged" victims whose deaths were inscribed at all.

of the jail. In it, were several Falangists with the fateful list. The prison official, Don Antonio, who was meticulous in the performance of his duties, demanded an official communiqué from the authorities before turning over the prisoners. The immediate response was to threaten him at gunpoint and to demand that he not oppose their orders or they would put him in the truck too.

"But gentlemen," poor Don Antonio told them, "understand that I am the responsible party here."

"That was under the old laws. Now there are only military orders which no one—do you understand?—no one can disobey," one of the criminals told him.

The news spread like a bombshell through the town. Mothers, fathers, brothers, and all the family members of those arrested hurried to the doors of the jail and the Creoli Cinema to learn the fate of their loved ones. Some brought bottles of coffee; others brought changes of clothing, any excuse to be there. It is said there was a strong barricade of local Falangists there. What shamelessness! People were allowed through one by one. Those who were told, "Your son, your father, or your brother has been taken to Huelva," understood at once the extent of the tragedy. Immediate cries of pain. That is why Juanilla Guzmán ran through the streets shouting, "Criminals, criminals!" She was lucky they didn't put her in jail, and from there, who knows. . . ? They say she had an uncle, a butcher by trade like his brother, who was in the Falange. By a strange twist of fate, this gentleman had a son studying in Madrid who had just died while serving as a lieutenant in the Republican army.

When, from one of the houses, there could be heard loud cries of grief for the assassination of a loved one, a pair of Falangists would arrive and, banging on the doors and windows with their rifle butts as a warning, would order the family members of the victim to be quiet. I remember that before the military coup, the town's jail would go for months and months without a single prisoner. It was the town with the smallest number of delinquents in Spain for its size.

The following night, no one in the town slept. On all of the street corners in the vicinity of the jail, there were indiscreet observers who wanted to see what would happen next. And the terror, a terror that weighed like lead on one's chest, invaded the town during those terrible nights during the bloody month of August 1936. The young men from "respectable" families, dressed in their Falangist uniforms, took it upon themselves to clear the curious observers from the area around the plaza where the jail and the town hall were located. The area was patrolled by Cleto, the bugler from the Civil Guard. He was accompanied by young men from some of the town's "best" families. There were the notary public's sons, Acuña's sons, Ramón Delgado's sons, Jacinta's sons, and Rosa's sons. Rosa, who was the daughter of Nene, the man with a scar on his lip. There was even a certain Manolito, known as 'Little Car.' The pain and fear of the family members of the hundreds of prisoners was so great that the presence of some witness was inevitable whenever fresh victims were taken from the jail. For that reason, the authorities decided to turn off the streetlights in the area around the plaza.

As I said, on the second night of the massacres no one in the town slept. That is the way it was. The Falangist executioners' truck arrived, smelling of gunpowder. Some entered the jail, where all the prisoners are shaking with fear. In the corridor or entranceway, a Falangist reads in a loud voice the names of those to be taken away.

"José Márquez Freire," he shouted.

A trembling voice responded, "Present."

He was immediately handcuffed and, with the barrel of a rifle pressed to the nape of his neck, was taken to the truck, where civil guards and other insurgents were waiting. Then came the second name, "José Álvarez Gómez." And the same procedure as before took place. One by one they were taken away, half dead already, to swell the unlucky group. The last one on the list was a navy motorman, Juan José Flores Val, a big strong lad who was brought up on the coast. He began punching all those he could reach, shouting, "Criminals, come fight me one by one. You're not going to kill me like a dog!"

A few seconds later, a rifle butt to the back of the neck left him sprawled unconscious on the floor. His was the twenty-fourth name on the list. It took six Falangists to lift him up and toss him into the truck, which left with its cargo in what would be another monstrous crime. A half hour later, they were assassinated among the pine trees.

The following day, new cries of pain again filled the cobblestone streets of that small white town. The neighbor women cautiously watched through partially opened doors and windows as the family members of those who had been executed passed by. Executions without trials, without tribunals, without defense attorneys. One could read in the newspapers, "A group of workers from this locale have been found dead. The perpetrators of the deed are unknown." And since I have spoken of the second night of the massacres and of Juan José Flores Val, known by his nickname 'El Misiño,' I want to record in my notes the news that the good Serafín passed on to me: a truck loaded with sacks of flour was coming from the nearby town of Villablanca on its way to Carro's bakery, located in our town, when they saw a severely wounded man on the highway. The driver got out and the wounded man, lying almost on the edge of the highway, asked him for water. The driver told him he had none but would go find some. When the truck arrived at its destination and unloaded the flour, the driver told what he had seen. From the bakery, the tale was relayed to the Falange headquarters and an automobile set out at once with four of those outlaws, who, upon arriving at the spot, administered the *coup de grace*: a shot in the back of the neck. That is how Juan José, 'El Misiño,' died, murdered in this cowardly fashion.

It is calculated that, by now, more than two hundred people have been executed, some eighty from the town and the rest peasants from the towns of the province who, according to international law, sought refuge in Portugal. They were arrested by the border guards and immediately turned over to the Spanish insurgents, who tied their hands with wires and brought them back and killed them on the outskirts of the town. Needless to say, the Portuguese consul in Ayamonte, taking advantage of the turbulence, took it upon himself to hunt down Portuguese refugees who had come to Spain to escape the dictatorship of Oliveira Salazar, and who now took off for parts unknown. One Portuguese refugee who was vilely assassinated was Arturo Pessoa, who had a mechanic's shop in our town.

Today, Serafín has brought a copy of *Odiel,* the provincial newspaper, which should be called *Odio* [Hate], for the venom its pages distill. There I have read of the executions of our dear friends and comrades: the lawyer

Don Juan Gutiérrez Prieto, a parliamentary deputy; Diego Jiménez Castellano, the civil governor of Huelva; and all the Republican authorities of the province. It was an act that took place to the accompaniment of bugles and drums in Punta del Cebo, in Huelva.[11] I have read the entire newspaper. There was an article about my execution signed by José Pérez Bautista. I know him well. But I am still alive. Perhaps when this storm has passed, we will run into each other. The most extraordinary thing in the aforementioned newspaper is a list of norms from which I quote the following lines: "Our tactic should be the same as the one we employed in North Africa, the tactic by which we execute five percent of the population, leaving the remainder so paralyzed by terror that they will never rise up against us."[12]

I still cling to my idea that we are confronted by criminals, bestial men whose barbarism infects the rest of the town.

Serafín had just left my room and gone downstairs, when a formation of Portuguese airplanes passed. A group of Falangists had entered the bakery, asking Chanoca if he had a radio, because if he did, he should immediately hand it over at the town hall. Since this happened at the same time the airplanes were approaching, they decided to climb the stairway to my room to watch the planes go by. Alert to the danger and as swiftly as a feline, I climbed through

[11] The author confuses the place of execution with the place where some of those mentioned were arrested. The executions of the civil and military authorities took place in El Conquero. Furthermore, the assassination of the deputy Juan Gutiérrez Prieto took place a week after that of the provincial authorities, who were executed on August 4, 1936.

[12] Although the possibility exists that a text of this sort could be found in the press at the time, it should be said that this text has yet to be seen. The members of the Press Censorship Bureau would have to have been very lax that day to allow the publication of such a declaration. It is possible that Miguel Domínguez Soler transformed something he had heard into something he had read.

the window whose iron bars we had removed, ran across the rooftop terraces, and lay down behind one of the border walls, about fifty centimeters high. I put my hand on my pistol, caressing its handle, and waited. The Falangists also emerged from the window and stood on the terrace, watching the airplanes go by. Then they left the same way they had come. I breathed a deep sigh of relief because that could have been the end of my story.

Chanoca, who had remained downstairs with his wife Rosa, was trembling with fear, because if I had been discovered, they too would have suffered the consequences, especially with two sons being held in the jail. The scare is over, but I have to look for a way to survive this distressing situation. One day or another, I could be caught.

It is difficult to find a way out. The options are to cross into Portugal, enemy territory, and hide until the beasts have had their fill, or else cross the sea. I have a good boat. With water and provisions I could get to the African coast. The sail is magnificent and I know how to handle it like an expert. The hard part is to outrun the Spanish customs guards stationed on Isla Canela, with their swift launch, on the lookout for boats leaving the mouth of the River Guadiana. They demand maritime safe-conduct passes to prevent all attempts at escape.

To make matters worse, in that sector, the patrol is under the command of an infamous customs guard corporal who was driven out of this town by a violent popular protest over the killing of an alleged smuggler who was sailing in neutral waters. Their speedboat has powerful guns. If the mayor of that island could lay the groundwork for my escape, I would send him my boat "Rosita" with a fisherman who trolls those waters. Serafín is going to make discreet inquiries to see if my idea has a chance.

They have told me that the elderly, anticlerical Freemason Don Norberto Gómez was taken by car, accompanied by his wife and daughter, both fanatical Catholics, and made to kneel and pray before the image of Christ in repentance for his sins. Later, together with Salvador Morlera and other members of the Ayamonte Masonic Lodge, he was arrested and taken to the Puerto de Santa María Penitentiary.[13] That is where they are sending those venerable and peace-loving citizens who belong to that misunderstood philanthropic, philosophical, and progressive Institution. The Lodge was built in Salvador Morlera's patio on Cavalga Street, as we all knew.[14] Serafín has told me that shortly before the Fascists took the town, the local right-wing political boss had broken into the Lodge and confiscated all of the books and documents to destroy them, because his son was mistakenly enrolled as a Freemason. Once those documents disappeared, the boss's son would go on to become a Falangist through and through, and the leader of a Falangist militia unit with *carte blanche* to arrest unlucky workers.

---

13 Norberto Gómez Morlera, who became mayor of Ayamonte during the Republic, died like so many others in one of the most overcrowded prisons of the postwar, Puerto de Santa María.
14 The Lodge officers in January 1936 were: Domingo Massoni González (Worshipful Master), Antonio Mateo Alarcón (First Warden), José García Rosa (Second Warden), Pablo Ojeda Ojeda (Orator), Manuel Chacón García (Secretary), Salvador Morlera Ríos (Treasurer), Florencio Susino González (Master of Ceremonies), Eduardo Morán Romero (Steward), Antonio Vázquez Sánchez (Tyler), Manuel Villegas González (Historian), and José Mateos García (Almoner).

The Killings Continue

The searches and arrests continue. The beasts have yet to satiate their hunger for flesh and blood. Today they have found a municipal policeman named Antonio Barroso, 'The Flea,' hidden in a cistern; and in a closet, Wenceslao Ríos, an urban guard. They have taken them to the Civil Guard barracks, and from there, to the Falange headquarters. The latter is located in what had been the Workers' Center, headquarters of the socialist General Workers' Union. There is a priest there to confess those to be killed.

The insurgents have established a kitchen in the Falange headquarters for the members of this paramilitary organization. The meals are prepared by the mother of 'The Planter,' a member of the local committee of the Communist Party, sought high and low by 'The Thunderclap.' This poor mother summons all her courage to flatter the enemy and perhaps save her son if he is caught. Meanwhile, 'The Planter,' armed with a good rifle, is in hiding in the neighborhood where he lives and where they pass him the food and news he needs. Days later, they broke into the house. He was shaving, with his rifle on the table. Falangists aimed their rifles at him through the window. He came out with his hands up and they handcuffed him and took him to the jail. He asked for paper and a pen to write down his declaration and whatever might help him in his defense. Chanoca says he spent three days and nights implicating half the town.

"In what?" I said. "Of what wrongdoing can he accuse anyone? No one here has committed murder or attempted murder or even robbery."

"The fact is," Chanoca continued, "that when he finished writing his accusation, and on the advice of his mother, who visited him in jail, he got ready and they took him to the church to marry the woman with whom he was living. And it is said that they gave him hope that they would set him free if he enlisted in the Legion, which he accepted to save his skin. From the church, they took him back to his cell where a young man, a boy actually, Eliseo Garlito, secretary of the Socialist Youth organization, and also under arrest, treated him like a traitor and a scoundrel."

That same night, at exactly twelve o'clock, the truck of death arrived at the door of the jail. A moment of panic and emotion. There was a terrifying silence. The Falangist whose turn it was began to read in a loud voice the names that were written on the list. The first was 'The Planter.' Overjoyed, he gathered his blanket and things, thinking they were about to set him free. "Every man for himself," he said. When he emerged from the cell, he found himself confronted by rifle barrels. His face became contorted with desperation and he threw himself to the ground, crying like a baby, and said, "Where are you taking me?"

The second to be called was Eliseo Garlito, who emerged from the cell with great courage and a loud "Present!" It is said that he told 'The Planter,' "Let's die, you coward, like men who love an idea." Also taken away that night was 'The Flea,' who had already been beaten in the Falange headquarters; also Wenceslao, 'The Mountain,' and others, until a total of twenty-four would go to swell the extensive list of martyrs. At dawn, on the other side of the forest, the cadavers appeared, those of the cowardly as well as those of the brave. Wailing and lamentations everywhere. At times, the cries of pain would break one's heart. There is not a single dress or suit in the town that is not black. Everyone wears mourning attire. Fathers, mothers, brothers, children, and family members of those sacrificed make up the totality of the little white town.

I no longer sleep. I merely close my eyes and rest. My entire nervous system is upset and I jump like a hare at any noise. Aunt Rosa, Chanoca's wife, is at the door of the bakery, and her husband by the oven. When the Falangist patrol approaches up Galdames Street, she sounds the alert, and her husband or Serafín, with the handle of a long shovel, bangs the ceiling under my room to warn me of danger. I don't turn on the light for any reason. In the darkness, I exercise to stretch my legs. My appetite is good.

The infamy has struck even here. On one of those terrifying nights, Angelito, one of Chanoca's sons, who were being held at the jail, is taken away.[15] He had fallen, and it is not known where they took him to be buried. His father is in a rage. Rosa was a sea of tears. She and I have taken Chanoca to the upstairs room, advising him not to shout because, in addition to my life, that of their other son, José, arrested since the beginning of the Movement, also

---

15 Ángel Pérez Chanoca, seventeen years old and a baker by trade, was assassinated on August 20, 1936, according to the Civil Registry. The cause of death was "Having fallen during the Movement to save Spain."

hangs in the balance. I have already told him that we are up against a band of well-armed outlaws with all power in their hands. Any act of insubordination, any liberty taken, would lead us to be snuffed out like flies.

Last night, Diego Carrasco, better known as 'The Friar,' was found in San Francisco Alley, riddled with bullets. There are those who heard his cries of pain before he died. He said, "Criminal, my ghost will follow you as long as you live." And in the darkness, all that could be heard were the gunshots and the oaths of vengeance from that hulk of a man who earned his living with the little café he owned. Sometimes, with the café closed to all but a few friends, he conducted séances during which he acted as the medium. He shouted out the name of his murderer, which was heard by all those who lived on San Francisco Alley.

Among the cadavers that appeared in the area surrounding the town, it happened that one of them, which horrified the inhabitants, was that of the Socialist councilman Fernando Flores Domínguez, who was an expert builder. His body appeared on the cemetery terrace during one of those dawns full of red sun and blood. It had been riddled with bullets and lay in a pool of blood on the white bricks. They left him there all day, exposed to the August sun. On his chest they had placed a sign which said, "For having manifested his glee over the proximity of a red submarine." It happened that someone, a fisherman, saw a submarine belonging to the Republican government that was keeping watch over the sandbar between Spain and Portugal. When Fernando heard the news, he publicly expressed his happiness. For this deed, he was denounced and fell into the hands of this new inquisition.

During subsequent killings, Luciano, 'The Botfly,' lost his life, as well as Claudio Sánchez, 'The Wool,' and his wife, and many other people I knew. Simple union members or affiliates of some political party frowned upon by the reactionaries. And it is the town's "rich kids," the Acuña brothers, the son of the woman known as 'The Keel,' the son of 'Linda's Gimp,' Ramón Delgado's sons, René's son, the son of 'Scar Lip,' the Notary's son, 'The Thunderclap,' and others like them who break into the houses of the poor with their blue overalls and yellow belts and shoulder straps, smelling of dried blood and gunpowder. They are in league with the priests and military men, in other words, the cross and the sword, who are going to celebrate an open air mass in the plaza where the town hall is located. They wanted to celebrate the triumph of the insurgent generals. All the town's residents attend: some because they have a family member in the jail, and others who put in an appearance out of terror. Almost no one out of faith or because they want a victory for those who were demonstrating what beasts they were.

Deceit

Everyone wants to stay alive. No one wants to help us in any way. There are those who seek refuge and find nothing but excuses, because "whoever hides a fugitive will meet the same fate as him." Since the death of their son Ángel, the Chanoca family seems to want me to go away. I think they are right. I am putting these people who have behaved so generously in danger. I have spoken with Chanoca today. He answered me curtly, "All of you are to blame."

"Why?" I responded.

And he went on to say, "Before the bigwigs fled, they left a list of names in the town hall of the people they were going to kill, and this list has been useful to the others to lay the foundation for their vengeance."

It left me perplexed. I could only mumble, "That is a lie. It is impossible. Deaths and executions were never mentioned by the town's authorities. They even prevented an attempt to attack those who were being held in the jail. On the contrary, those people were protected and respected, and none of the leaders of this honorable town have ever conceived of the idea of liquidating enemies."

The fact of the matter is that, days later and in every town in the province, those enemies had used this deceit to justify their criminal conduct. There were those who were completely apolitical and were told by our enemies, "You have to help the Movement. You too were on the lists." And that peaceful and good citizen would become all worked up when told this tale of the famous and imaginary list.

Every morning, a group of workers and builders are taken from the jail and, escorted by Falangists, go to repair the damage caused by "reds" in the churches. In this way, the Falangists placate the fury of the ferocious and vindictive priests. This brings to mind what happened at the beginning. When news of the military coup reached the town, the people, en masse, headed to the churches to vent their rage by destroying every saint and image: symbols of an idolatry that had no reason to still exist so far into the twentieth century. On the evening of that first day, I was in the town hall, sitting with the Chief of the Border Police, who said to me, "What do you think of today's events?"

I responded, "It is best that it happened the way it did. The town's disapproval of the military coup is so evident that it has vented its rage breaking saints and idols. But images can be replaced, lives cannot."

"You are right," that functionary told me.

During the spontaneous and public demonstration, there wasn't a single act of aggression, not a single person injured. The wives of the absent civil guards who had gone off to join the insurrection were not bothered or shown disrespect, nor were their children. Those alleged to have contacts with the insurgents were arrested under governmental orders. That is the worst that the "reds" did. And it was to repay this noble behavior, to repay this respect for human life, that these beasts on the prowl committed mass murder against hundreds of workers who one day protested because they were hungry.

Eliminating us was their solution to the unemployment problem. They did not kill on Fridays. They say that as good Christians and out of respect for Christ, who died on a Friday, on that day they abstain from the daily massacre.

Exposed

I have summoned the courage to climb through the window of the room where I am hiding, scramble across rooftop terraces and down to the door of the house belonging to the women we used to call 'The Canners.' There I encounter Isabel Soler and express my condolences for the death of her sister Carmen, assassinated in one of the first massacres. Isabel told me, "We are not afraid."

I asked her, "In case the Falangists break in, is there a backdoor or window so I can escape?" She answered in the negative. "Then I will stay only a few minutes."

Isabel told me how her sister Carmen died together with Nemesia and Martina Álvarez. "Martina," she said, "died with her fist raised high, shouting, 'Criminals! I die for an idea and so that my daughter will know a better world.'" I asked her if she was prepared to take up a rifle in the event governmental troops landed or approached, and she told me she was. I took my leave of Isabel and clambered up a low wall, and from there to the terrace.

I have returned to Chanoca's house. The baker Serafín has seen me and told me I was crazy for undertaking such an unwise adventure. "You barely escaped being caught. At this very moment, the Falangists are conducting a house to house search of the street where you were. They are looking for articles taken from the churches. Don't try anything like that again." His words still echo in my ears: "It would be better if you went over to the Moors." It is a very old saying in this part of Spain for people persecuted by the Inquisition who fled overland or across the sea, passing over to the enemy. As if that were not bad enough, I have been told that a firing squad composed of Assault Guards has arrived in town and are being lodged in several private houses.

As to my plan to escape in my boat "Rosita," I have been informed that it is impossible. The mayor of Isla Canela has been arrested and surveillance along the coast has been increased for fear of a landing by the Republican navy. No one without a maritime safe-conduct pass can get through. Our friends said that if governmental forces landed, neither you—they were referring to me—nor anyone could hold us back. Each family would take justice into their own hands. "The criminals will not escape the ire of the people." Those poor, unwary citizens had taken out their anger on saints and figurines. Lives were respected. Everyone asked themselves the reason for this terrible repression.

A sunny month of August with cadavers, dried blood covering the faces, lying among the pine groves without family members to gather them up and give them a decent burial because these victims' whereabouts are unknown. After being left exposed to the sun to spread terror among passersby, they are taken in trucks to towns like Villablanca, San Silvestre, or Lepe. Among the scores of sad and moving scenes, one remembers the case of a driver named Espinosa who was forced to go with a truck to the pine groves to gather cadavers with perforated craniums and deposit them in cemeteries, whose locations he was told to keep absolutely secret. Imagine his surprise when this driver found among the dead his own brother Ángel, who had been brought there from a considerable distance to be executed. The horrible and bitter scene cannot be adequately described in a few words.

There is also the case of the man known as 'Linda's Gimp'—actually, one of his legs had been amputated—who did not belong to any party or union, and earned his living with his hands, repairing tires. He was under arrest. They say he had been going from tavern to tavern and, horrified by the bloodletting carried out by the Fascists, he could not hold back his pain, hatred, and virile nature, and would shout, "Criminals! Assassins!" Since he had a son in the Falange, all they did was arrest him, but there in the jail he witnessed the daily horror of those taken away to be shot and he began shouting even louder. One day, they took him away in the truck of death to a pine grove and placed him among the condemned. When they fired, they killed everyone but him. Then they put him back in the truck and brought him back to the jail, thinking he would be terrified into keeping quiet, but it was all in vain. They carried out this operation twice. Finally, they had to kill him.

What General Yagüe Said

It was published in the newspapers: "I don't want to leave a single enemy at my back." That is why people were saying that the life of a human being is worth less than that of a dog. In the past, during these hot days and calm nights, the peaceful residents used to gather in the streets, seated on their cane chairs or on mats of woven reeds or grass, and spend hours and hours telling old stories until well into the wee hours of the morning. During these tragic days, the doors are hermetically sealed. Silence and terror has taken hold of this most noble and loyal town. Inside, only the infants sleep.

At times, one hears voices in some street. When a rifle butt bangs loudly on some door, the whole street is on alert, ears pressed to windows and doors, people asking themselves, "Where is it?" When the door is opened, those who make up the band of outlaws break in, without respect or any sense of shame, treating the inhabitants as if they were animals or some inferior species. People who, under the circumstances, have no more rights than a slave. In the twentieth century. The ironies of destiny.

Sometimes, one heard a voice saying, "My husband has never been involved in anything," or "My son hasn't done anything." And in the wee hours of the morning, beneath the stars, some unlucky citizen is taken away in handcuffs, perhaps because they had expressed their annoyance over what was happening while they were in some café or within earshot of some anonymous person who denounced them.

Tonight, the first of September, I have taken stock of my situation. It has been thirty-three days since the Fascists took over the town. That adds up to so many days of torment for me that I have no choice but to risk everything once and for all. I have dressed up as a woman. Black skirt, black blouse, and a black kerchief on my head. This is what is worn by all the women. The stores are sold out of black dye to turn colored clothes into mourning attire. I have been told that the president of the Socialist Youth organization, Sebastián Casillas, whose father was assassinated, was hiding in a brothel known as "The Peasant Woman's House." Sebastián was a little younger than me, and I have gotten it in my head that together we could sail due south into the Atlantic for six days and then veer east to the part of the Moroccan coast controlled by the French. We would either die or triumph. I have a rifle with sixteen rounds hidden under a nearby fence, and my ever-present pistol.

It is midnight. Not a single sound or conversation can be heard. Chanoca has told me, "If you leave here, you cannot come back. You know by now that we love you very much, but we are afraid you might be followed." I had already thanked him for the enormous sacrifice of sheltering me, but it has been twenty nights since I have managed to sleep. I must prepare myself to find a definitive solution for my desperate situation, as unpleasant for me as for them. He asked me, "Where are you going?" I replied, "I will tell you later."

In front of the bakery was the steep street where the schoolhouse was. At the top of that climb is the road to the cemetery. I headed downhill to San Francisco Alley precisely where Diego Carrasco had been killed. There was a hedge of agave plants. From the corner of the alley I could see Duarte, the famous corporal of the municipal police who had been dismissed during the Republic. Armed with a rifle, he was standing guard further down the street, under the lights of the soap factory, to prevent anyone from taking that way out to the countryside. Suddenly, I heard footsteps coming down San Francisco Alley and jumped over the agave hedge as Duarte readied his rifle. A short while later, someone appeared. It was my friend Jerónimo, who was going to see his fiancée Paquita, who lived on the other side of town. Duarte stopped him and asked if he had seen anyone in the alley. When he told him he hadn't, Duarte told him, "I am waiting for one we are going to give it to good." From what I could hear, I realized he was referring to me.

Further up the alley, shots rang out. "They are killing someone in that direction," I said to myself and, like a coward, I had to give up my attempt as a lost cause. It was only by luck I had not been killed. The Falangists were installing a new heavy machine gun across from the textile factory on the road to the cemetery, right where I would have had to pass. There must have been thirty or forty insurgents congregated there, among them Falangists, civil guards, and Carlist militiamen. There would have been no way to protect myself. And I was a mere forty meters away.

A New Hiding Place

"One more day and still alive," I said to myself. Taking every precaution and returning by the same route I had come, I got to Chanoca's bakery. As usual, the door was open. Serafín greets me. He has told me that at my fiancée's house, everything was prepared. Her father, a member of the Socialist Party, had built me a magnificent hiding place in an attempt to save me. My fiancée's house had no rear exit. It was located on a stony slope across from the bakery. Since things are going from bad to worse, I sent Serafín to deliver the news of my arrival and, minutes later, I entered. Behind the door, left ajar, they were waiting for me with joy and sorrow. Sorrow for the circumstances of our encounter.

The hiding place consisted of the hollow for an interior window some eighty centimeters tall and, with the thickness of the wall, some sixty centimeters deep. It was one of those old-fashioned houses where an interior room only received light from an adjacent outer room through such windows. The exterior side was covered by a cupboard full of plates and glasses. On the inside, my fiancée's father had hung a wooden door on two hinges. All well-disguised. To cover up where the wood and the wall met, there were coat hooks with clothing hanging from them. When the door was open, it was supported by two cords which, once I had entered the hiding place, I would pull from the inside in order to close it. It caused me some anguish that, once inside, I was truly caught in a trap with no means of escape. There was a light bulb in the room, but I cut the wires to the switch so it could not be turned on. In the room, there was a bed with a mattress, and in the center of the room, a large box full of netting for mackerel fishing. I have tried to sleep a little but, with my eyes closed, I hear everything that is happening around me.

I was lying on the bed when there was a loud pounding on the door and a booming voice that said, "Open up for the military authorities."

My fiancée's father answered, "One moment."

My fiancée hurriedly rolled up the mattress while I climbed into my hiding place. I was frightened but felt calm. With one hand, I held the cord to the trapdoor, and with the other, I took out my pistol, released the safety, and put my finger on the trigger. They entered and I recognized the voice of 'The Thunderclap' when he said, "We have come for Miguel."

My fiancée's mother was the first to answer: "We have heard nothing from him for a long time now."

"Fine," one of them said. "We are going to search the house."

"Is there a well or cistern?" another said.

"No sir," they replied.

Then began the insults and threats. They stabbed mattresses and opened closets and, finally, came to the end of the house where I was hidden. They entered my interior room and ordered my fiancée's father to remove the fishnets. Thick drops of sweat rolled down my forehead. I held my breath. 'The Thunderclap' asked, "Who sleeps in that bed?"

My fiancée's mother answered, "Miguel."

And they told her, "If he shows up here, do not let him in, because if you shelter him, you will all be killed."

Since my fiancée's father was still removing the fishnets, one of them told him, "Do that carefully and gladly, because it is a command from the military authorities."

Another said, "The wires for the light have been cut."

My fiancée's mother replied, "Yes, my husband cut them because the room smelled as if there were a short circuit."

I continued to sweat and could feel the drops falling from my forehead. I was suffocating. I became dizzy. I was on the verge of passing out. I felt like killing and being killed. If they try to move the cupboard, I am lost. Finally, they left the room. They have sat down around the kitchen table. Through a crack in the cupboard, I can see that 'The Thunderclap' has his back toward me. He lights a cigarette. Addressing my fiancée, he said, "Don't count on your fiancé anymore. One day or another, he will be arrested, and I warn all of you that if he comes to this house, don't put him up, because if we catch him here, you will all pay the price." After these menacing words, 'The Thunderclap' got up and began to leave. One by one, they all left. I heard the door bolt slide into place and I began to relax my grip on the cord that held the trapdoor shut. I took a deep breath.

The danger has passed. My fiancée has told me there were eleven of them altogether. They are looking for me to kill me. I ask myself why. I haven't killed or attacked anyone. Have these dangerous people taken a potion that turns them into beasts? A dead man is no longer of any use to the cause of liberty and justice. I have lived in a world of poverty and I thought the solution for humanity lay in the creation of a society based on cooperation. Life and wealth could be found in cooperatives where we would all be owners and workers. It is monstrous that they would kill me like a dog for thinking this way. Only a man who is alive could continue to plant the seeds for a better world. I intend to stay alive.

Having emerged from my hiding place, I see my fiancée with her arms crossed, kneeling before a picture of the Virgin surrounded by souls, under which an oil lamp was burning. Isabel was crying and praying. Later, we talk in low voices. The doors and windows have ears. The terror, the great terror celebrated in the provincial newspaper *Odiel*, was the emperor of that tragic time.

Another day of death deferred has dawned on my life as a fugitive. An impossible thought simmers in my mind: how I could start a popular uprising. Without arms, we would be defeated, and all those in the jail or the Creoli Cinema would be taken out and exterminated without pity. Was there no way out of this mire? My future sister-in-law, the diminutive Carmela, with other girls her age, went to the cemetery. When she came back that afternoon, she related the following story: "The gravedigger is making a hole big enough to bury fourteen men, among them Miguel. They have thirteen locked up in the jail and are waiting to arrest him at any moment, in order to hold the first public execution against the cemetery wall." The girl, who did not know I was in the house, broke into sobs. "Do you think, Sister, that they will find him?"

The Humiliating Parade

That execution was going to be the talk of the town. Intellectuals and men of the middle class were going to fall before the rifles of the assault guards as the whole town watched. There is no point in even imagining what that would have been like, the spectacle of watching the assassination of loved ones who had never harmed a soul. After days went by and I did not appear, they came for my fiancée's father who, by a cruel twist of fate, was named José Domínguez just like my father, and placed him against the wall around the Borreguero orchard, as if they were going to execute him.

"We will spare your life if you tell us where Miguel is."

The poor man, who had my life in his hands as the expression goes, answered, "Kill me if you like, but we do not know where he is hiding."

Finally, after a brief consultation among the executioners, they put him in the car and drove him back to town. They say it was the notary's son who was in charge of that platoon of bandits.

The harassment of my fiancée's family would not end there. Two Falangists came in search of Isabel's mother. They have taken her to the Falange headquarters, which had belonged to the General Workers' Union and the Socialist Party. There were already thirty-five or forty other terrified women there: the wives, mothers, sisters, or daughters of "runaways." That was their label for us: "the runaways." Falangists, armed to the teeth, kept watch over the terrified women while poor Toribio Valencia cut off their hair, his hand trembling as it worked the scissors. He had been forced to commit this atrocity. Tears and sobs filled the large hall. They were all honorable women. Some were made to drink a large quantity of castor oil, and then a procession was organized with the women marching down the center of the street, and the Falangists lined up on the sidewalks. That was the beginning of a parade along every street in the town. Some women tried to wipe away their tears or cover their faces with their aprons. In response, one of those savages would strike them on the hands with a rifle butt. The "procession of shame," led by drums and bugles, passed along the street in front of our house, and no one, in the face of that horror, went out to see the terrible spectacle. Isabel and Carmela cried bitterly. "That is where they are taking Mamá," said Carmela. And I, who could hear it all, felt as though I would go crazy that day.

The sun was setting when the poor woman came home. In her body, which barely measured a meter and a half, she had nerves and a will of steel. She came in saying, "No need to worry. Why get upset? Because of my hair? It will grow out soon enough and, if not, we can buy a wig. I am not afraid."

The Executions

It was five o'clock in the afternoon on that day when I was supposed to have died. From my hiding place, I heard the rifles' discharge and then the *coups de grace*. I could barely breathe with the rage that filled my whole body. I had not been able to do anything for the victims. All I achieved was to postpone that public massacre a few days because they couldn't find me.

This is how the drama unfolded. The truck was waiting at the door of the jail. They took out Pedrito Gutiérrez; Salvador Feu; the schoolteacher, Don Manuel Chacón Díaz; Romualdo Herrera, 'Little Vine'; and Bruno Alonso Calvo, who used to manage the Port's signal lights. They loaded them handcuffed into the truck, where they were watched over by assault guards. The truck set out along Rivera Street and then up Buenavista Street in the direction of the cemetery. It was four-thirty in the afternoon. The town trembled in fear. The women, horrified, closed the doors of their houses.

"When those men were taken away, they were already more dead than alive," the people said. They lined them up against the wall. The rabble came to attend the executions, and a large contingent of Falangists and civil guards formed a barrier to hold back the curious. A few meters from the wall, the firing squad formed. When the time came, they fired their rifles. Before he fell, Salvador Feu, secretary of the local Communist Party, mustered the strength to shout, "Long live the Soviet Union!" That bitter hour had ended, taking away the lives of thirteen people, some because they were Freemasons and others because the criminal "Movement" did not tolerate their political ideologies. They were cleansing the rearguard of those who might be enemies in the event of a hypothetical revenge. But they were entirely mistaken. It is impossible to stop the normal course of social justice and progress.

I am still alive. Destiny has saved me for something else. They have assigned to Señor Juan el de Castillo the task of guarding the house. He sits on the doorstep with his rifle resting between his legs, waiting for my arrival. The fact of the matter is that I am already inside.

The Leader of the Coup Pays Us a Visit

General Queipo de Llano has come to the town. Mothers and family members of those locked up in the jail or the cinema come and kneel before him. This bigwig told them, "We do not kill anyone. Only those with blood on their hands will be tried." How many among the hundreds of unlucky souls that you have assassinated had blood on their hands? That was the strategy of these murderers in all the towns of my beloved Andalusia. I still have the words of *Odiel* engraved on my retinas: "by killing five percent of the population. . . ." Already the remainder of the population is more than terrified. That is what the circumstances demanded. Queipo de Llano could stroll through the town which, lifeless and defenseless, has been cowed and emasculated by fear.

Everything goes from bad to worse. The news from Río Tinto is unfavorable. A column of Moorish and foreign mercenaries, supported by a company of Portuguese "Viriatos," has landed in Huelva and are heading to Río Tinto, where the strongest focus of resistance is located, and another column has crossed the Portuguese border further north to cut off the miners from the rear.

Flight

I can stand it no longer. I am compromising this magnificent family. My own parents could not have done more for me. We discussed it, and my fiancée's parents and I formulated a plan for my escape that very night. I know that I will have to cross a kilometer and a half of the River Guadiana, and that it will not be easy. On this side, the customs guards keep watch, and on the other shore, there are the Police for the Protection and Defense of the State. And a small boat, even at night, is easy to spot. Fourteen hours remain until I have to expose myself in a life or death adventure.

The time arrived. It must have been two o'clock in the morning. Juan el de Castillo was dozing on the doorstep. My fiancée's mother, who worked as a baker and sold the wheat bread she kneaded, opened the door and asked Juan what time it was. He lit a match and looked at his watch. "It is two o'clock in the morning."

"Thank you," she replied, "I have to go knead my bread right away."

Ten minutes later, I emerged wearing a black petticoat and dressing gown the same as my fiancée's mother's, with my head covered by a black shawl and with a basket containing two jackets and shoes. I had summoned all my courage. I went a few meters and entered Chanoca's bakery. He and Serafín were aghast. I removed my black clothing, opened my shirt, and tucked my pistol away. I asked for a large basket like those used to deliver bread, and put my shoes and two jackets in it. With a total of seven pesetas in my pocket, I descended the street in the direction of the Concepción Bridge that crossed the river.

My fiancée's father had already placed two oars in a friend's boat. I only had to go two hundred meters. When I enter the alley between the Concepción building and the factory, I see a customs guard sitting on a sardine press in the semi-darkness. Sensing my presence, he lifted his head. The intense fear I was feeling made me draw my pistol and aim it at his head. We recognized each other at once.

"Miguel, are you crazy? Don't you know I have a wife and children?" he said.

"Give me your rifle and I won't have to kill you," I told him. I was trembling uncontrollably and a cold sweat drenched my forehead.

"I want to save myself. I want to live," I exclaimed. "I will leave your rifle on the bridge. Don't come looking for it until I am far away."

"May God protect you," he said.

I quickly deposited the rifle at the end of the bridge, jumped into the boat, and in a matter of seconds was rowing up the Guadiana. I did not go downstream toward the sea, because I knew that the customs guards who were watching the estuary would come out and capture me. As I row, I keep my eyes fixed on the bridge, barely visible in the darkness, and keep a steady rhythm, lifting the oars only a few centimeters above the surface of the river. I have angled out to the middle of the river where there is less danger of being seen. I shouldn't get too close to the Portuguese shore because they may have been notified of my escape by the Spanish authorities. Here, I am slightly illuminated by the light from the town. I don't reach total darkness until I have passed a bend in the river. There is no moon tonight. I have gotten through the most dangerous phase, but there is a patrol on the Portuguese shore. I can hear them speaking. They have seen my boat and think I am coming ashore. I head back toward the middle of the river. I hear them say, "*Vai para sima*." They are saying I am going upriver. Now I know where the enemy is and can take advantage of this moment when they have left their post.

A half hour later, I arrive at Zambujera Hill. It casts a dark shadow over a bend in the river. The basket with my shoes and clothing is in the boat. I accelerated my oar strokes, tied my shoes around my neck, put on both my jackets, and, a few meters from the shore, slid overboard and pushed my boat out into the river. The water is almost up to my chest, but, in spite of the muddy river bottom, I quickly reached the shore and set foot on Portuguese territory. Was I falling into a trap? So far, my plan had worked just as I had hoped. Now I must run and get away from the shore as quickly as possible. I set my course, guided by the stars. There is a ditch and then a tarred road. I cross it quickly. I have to go as far into the countryside as I can before the sun comes up. Finally, I reached a pine forest, removed my wet clothes and wringed them out, twisting them with all my strength. It was September and the weather was fairly mild.

Seated among the pine needles, I have reclined against one of those trees and an irresistible urge to sleep comes over me. I almost close my eyes when a tortoise that was in the tree brings me back to the reality of my situation. I realize that my feet are bleeding from the thorns in the woods I have traversed. Now, at dawn, I am intensely cold. Downhill from my hiding place, I see a well with a bucket next to the well's edge. I put on my pants and go down to wash the mud off my feet. I also clean out the puncture wounds from the thorns and then quickly return to where I have left the rest of my clothes. I hear gunshots everywhere and recall that this is opening day of the hunting season in Portugal.

My shirt and undershirt are still damp, but I have no alternative but to put them on. They will dry on my body. I have put my shoes on and I notice that my navy blue jacket's color has run, staining my grey jacket. The tobacco and rolling paper in my pouch are wet and I am desperate for a smoke. Finally the sun comes up and shines radiantly from the east. It brings welcome warmth. It is already ten o'clock in the morning and I have turned my back to the sun to dry myself well. I approached a small road that ran along the edge of the pine forest and was suddenly startled by the arrival of a man riding a mule. Upon seeing me, he stopped and, before I could speak, he understood my whole tragedy. He told me that the farms in the area were being patrolled by members of the Portuguese dictator Salazar's Republican Guards, hunting for fugitives. "Follow me if you wish," he said.

I don't hesitate. We have arrived at a hedgerow and he has told me to walk behind the tall thorny plants. After another kilometer, we come to a small house from which a woman emerged who became rather alarmed when she saw me. At the urging of her husband, she invited me in. They prepared me a cup of coffee with milk while I observed the abject poverty in which this couple lived. The man gave me a small packet of rolling papers. I had dried my tobacco on the stove. I smoked my first cigarette, which tasted like heaven to me. The cup of coffee and a piece of black bread made me feel better. I gave them a two peseta coin and my grey jacket, which they thanked me for.

The man said, "Now you must hide behind the house while I go notify a friend who lives nearby. You will be safer there than here."

I hid for almost half an hour until he returned. From my hiding place, I kept an eye on the road and saw him coming. Seeing he was alone, I approached him. He gave a hand signal for me to follow. In this way, we covered two hundred meters with the good fortune not to be seen by anyone. We entered a large farm and he told me, "Hide under that fig tree." He shook my hand to say good-by and then went to the farmhouse to let them know I was there. In case of danger, I was planning a possible escape route through the lush fig trees, whose branches reached all the way to the ground.

A quarter of an hour later, I saw a small girl, about eighteen years old, coming my way. My heart began to beat with joy. It was Sebastiana Bento, the daughter of a landowner who had lived many years in Spain. Sebastiana had been born there, and when we were young, I had often danced with her. When she saw me, an astonished look came over her face and we immediately merged in an effusive embrace and smothered each other with kisses.

"My dear friend, how are you?" she said. I briefly explained everything I had been through. She told me that from here, the flashes of gunfire were clearly visible when the firing squads were at work.

Sebastiana has gone to prepare me something to eat. I remember this quiet family that used to live on a farm they had in the countryside outside our town, and where they kept a sizable herd of goats. Once, as a man to be trusted, I had had to defend Sr. Bento in court when the Civil Guard accused him of allowing his goats to graze among the pine groves belonging to the Marqués de Astorga. Since the accusations were nearly continual, he had to sell his goats and farm, and return to Portugal.

Sebastiana returned with a basket and a bottle of water. She brought boiled eggs, salt pork, chorizo, and a piece of bread. I wanted to sleep more than I wanted to eat, and asked her to bring me a blanket so I could sleep under the fig tree. She told me to eat, and that later, I could go to the house and sleep upstairs where there was a hayloft, because members of Salazar's Republican Guards, who were patrolling the border in search of fugitives, always came to rest or drink in the rooms downstairs. If they found me, they would return me in handcuffs to Spain. When night fell, Sebastiana came for me. I entered the house and there I was greeted by the family patriarch, Sr. Bento, who, on this occasion, did not shake my hand but instead gave me a warm embrace.

"Don't be afraid. You are as safe as if it were your own house. I will watch over you like a father." Those were his exact words. While we ate, and to my great shame, I began to cry. I related all that had happened, at which Bento grew increasingly indignant.

Sebastiana had prepared a pallet for me in the hayloft and commanded me to remove all my clothes, which she said were dirty, so she could wash them for me. I had no alternative but to obey my friend's orders. She took everything, washed it, and by dawn the next day, it was hanging in the sun behind the house. She brought me a large cup of coffee and milk and toasted bread with lard. I have already told her that I have slept the night before as if I had returned from the ends of the earth. Sebastiana and I are reminiscing about the happy days of the town's festivals with their open air dances. The music, the peace. And now, those who used to play soccer with me, who used to go on excursions along the placid waters of the river in my rowboat, those who had been great friends and were studying with me in the same school, were now serving unscrupulously as informers for the Fascist gangs.

Bento called to Sebastiana from downstairs. "Stay there until I bring your clothes," she told me. I have fallen back to sleep. I was wondering if Bento trusted the man who brought me to this farm, or if he had had to pay him to keep quiet until my escape could be arranged.

Before falling asleep, I think about the customs guard. That functionary's name was Fuentes. If he had wanted, I would not have escaped. It would have been easy for him to sound the alarm, and that swift launch with its powerful gun would have blown me away in the middle of the river. Luck is on my side. Today, my fairy godmother is Sebastiana. I hope my good fortune continues. I remember that Carmelita had said that they were going to kill fourteen of us, and then they would not kill anymore. So the beasts had satiated their hunger. They had had their fill.

About four in the afternoon, Sebastiana brought me my clothes, clean and ironed. As I dressed, she told me that at six o'clock in the morning on the following day, her father was going to take me to the Monte Gordo train station where he would give me directions to meet up with a person I know. The die is cast. In my wallet, I have the address of a relative of Isabel's father in Tavira. I am hoping to find him there.

I have gone downstairs where Bento was waiting for me. "Today," he told me, "is the Monte Gordo fair. The highway is full of livestock and horse traders. We are going to intermingle with that crowd. You will go on foot, holding my horse's bridle. Don't speak to anyone. Just keep your eyes on the ground and continue on your way." Bento had already bought me two packets of fine tobacco from Holland.

Sure enough, the highway was full of people and livestock. Bento rode slowly. Since he was an important landowner, many people approached to greet him. I was wearing a typical peasant's sombrero and kept my face hidden beneath its broad brim. We traveled in that manner for about a kilometer and a half until we arrived at the train station.

Bento took me to a corner of the station and told me, "Wait here for a minute."

Later, he returned with a train ticket and a railroad employee. "This man," said Bento, "is as much of a 'red' as you."

The man shook my hand and pointed to a stone wall about twenty meters from the station. Then he told me that the train wouldn't be coming until two o'clock in the afternoon and that I should hide behind that wall until he whistled to me three times. I followed his instructions exactly, sitting behind the wall with my back to the station. Bento had left. There wasn't even time to say good-by.

It was a few minutes to two when the railroad employee approached the wall and told me, "You are not going to get off in Tavira because the police are always on duty there to arrest suspicious-looking people. At the first stop, there is an unmanned train station called Porta Nova, a kilometer before Tavira. Get off there and to the right you will see a road that goes to Tavira. Eight hundred meters down that road is Almirante Reis Street. You already have the house number. It is up to you to find it." I thanked him and went to the station. Soon the train arrived. I looked up and the railroad employee motioned for me to approach. He took my straw sombrero and had me climb up into the car. Minutes later, I was on my way.

I sat next to a window, looking out so no one would see my face. The train stopped in Porta Nova and I got off quickly. So far everything was going as planned. I am on the road that will take me to the indicated street. It was not difficult to find, nor was the house. I knocked and the lady who was married to my fiancée's relative opened the door. The man's name was Agustín. He played in the Tavira municipal band. He was a master barber and very well-regarded. His wife sent one of the children to notify her husband while she, who appeared to be incredibly near-sighted, peeled a potato. From what I can observe, these people are very poor. Uncle Agustín arrived and told me to forgive him but he could only shelter me for a few minutes, because if I was found in his house, the two of us would be taken in handcuffs to Spain to be killed.

"Take it easy, friend, they are not killing people anymore. It is no big deal. I only want a glass of wine and something to eat. Here, take these five pesetas." I had told him the part about the killings being over in order to calm him down a bit. He left with the five pesetas and I became somewhat agitated by the thought that he might be capable of turning me in. Finally, he returned. He brought a bottle of wine and a ticket for a bus that was leaving within an hour for Olhâo, a fishing village on the Atlantic coast, but further from Spain. "Go to this address which belongs to my brother Pepe, and be very careful," he told me.

I drank a glass of wine and ate a few fried potatoes. We left at once. He went ahead and I followed from behind. When we got to a small square, the bus was there. I couldn't say good-by to him. He had vanished. I got onto the bus and the people watched me, some with compassion and others with distrust. For a few moments, I was feeling bitter about the awkward situation I was in. Finally, the bus departed and an hour later we had arrived in Olhâo. I got off quickly and asked the first person I met how to get to Rua da Liberdade, Liberty Street. It was getting dark. I had no problem finding the house. I knocked on the door and was greeted by a young woman about eighteen or twenty years old. While I was talking to her, another young woman came out. She was wearing glasses. In a few words, I explain that I am the fiancé of Cousin Isabel in Ayamonte. They invited me in and introduced me to Aunt Luisa, Uncle Pepe's wife. Although they were born in Portugal, the girls spoke correct Spanish. Once inside, I told them the story of my odyssey. We were sitting at a table lit by a kerosene lamp, because the house did not have electricity.

Uncle Pepe arrived, a big man who was bald and who made his living soldering tin cans at the sardine-packing plant. I explained to him everything I had already told the others. I gave him his brother Agustín's regards and he said, "Did you tell my brother all about what was going on in Spain?" I told him I had. "Well, my brother, as fearful as he is, will not be able to sleep for days. Don't be afraid here. If you haven't been followed, not even Jesus Christ knows where you are. I have a friend who is a smuggler who will give the family the news of your arrival. Do not worry."

I stood up and made a tour of the whole house, which had a patio with a ladder up to the roof terrace. I went up. I saw that the neighborhood consisted entirely of one-story houses, and that one could run from one terrace to another and even drop down to the adjoining streets. I explained why the situation made me uneasy. "Do not worry," Uncle Pepe told me again. The girls and Aunt Luisa had already set the table to eat. As almost every day in Portugal, there is fried fish today. I have excused myself and asked them to please give me a blanket and let me sleep. I feel as if I have a hundred and four degree fever. I have always suffered chronic throat infections and, after the soaking I got in the river, it is back.

They laid a mattress over a straw mat in a small room. There were no beds. They prepared an herbal tea for me. I lay down and they covered me up well. Cousin María, the one with the glasses, has brought me an aspirin. I wrote down a prescription for iodine and glycerin that Aunt Luisa could take to a pharmacy in the morning. I have found that a few dabs of it soothe my throat. My eyes begin to close. The nightmares that wake me are terrible. I dream of rose beds with sharp thorns that I can't pass through. Men with the faces of monsters appear and, armed with knives, try to catch me. Sweat flows from all my pores. I am exhausted and lack all strength. I want to sleep and never wake up. I feel my hands tensely clenching oars, until at last I fall into a deep sleep.

In the morning, I wake up and it all seems as if I had been a character in some novel. I feel better. I no longer feel the intense cold I have brought with me since my bus ride the day before. I get up, put my clothes on, and leave the room. Uncle Pepe and the girls are having breakfast before going to work. When they see me, they urge me to go back to bed. "I can't sleep anymore," I said and tied a handkerchief around my neck.

I think I have fallen in with a good family. They have gone off to their jobs. I stay in the house with Aunt Luisa, who is a seamstress and makes shirts for a store that provides her thread, buttons, and cloth. At the completion of each shirt, they give her a ridiculously small payment. Aunt Luisa has a dark complexion and is very thin. Cousin Dolores told me that her aunt had stomach problems. The girls are Uncle Pepe's nieces. His sister, the girls' mother, lives in Tavira with other children. Here in Olhâo, María and Dolores, who are well-educated, work in a lithography shop.

One of Uncle Pepe's pastimes is raising canaries, and Aunt Luisa was in charge of keeping their cages clean. Since this did not require a lot of work, I asked her to let me take over the chore of blowing away the birdseed shells, filling the feeder, as well as providing them water and scraping the cages clean. Then Aunt Luisa left for the pharmacy, locking the door as she left. "If someone knocks, don't open the door for anyone," she told me.

While she was gone, I busied myself arranging the ten or twelve cages with the variously colored canaries kept by Uncle Pepe. Aunt Luisa returned with a small jar of iodine and glycerin, and, with a small cotton swab, I dabbed a little on my tonsils.

"I've been thinking," she said, "since the girls have a brother more or less your age, we could have papers made for you with the name Agustín, just like the boy." It seemed like a magnificent idea to me. At dinner time, we must suggest it to the family. That way we could go out for walks together, and if questioned by the police, we could present them with the papers in Agustín's name. The only risk would be an inopportune encounter in the street with someone who knew me. There were groups of Spanish Fascists of both sexes who were in Portugal seeking help for the "Glorious" National Movement.

María and Dolores occasionally bought the newspaper *O Século*. There was a copy on a small table by the door. I have picked it up and read all the news about what was happening in Spain. The stories were completely distorted, accusing the "reds" of hundreds of crimes. They left me speechless. I realized I was in enemy territory.

I went into the patio, climbed the ladder to the roof terrace, and took a walk from terrace to terrace. The block of houses adjoined three streets. From the terraces to the street, there was a drop of about five meters.

"Magnificent," I said to myself, "jumping down to the street would be no problem." My leg muscles are like iron from all the cycling I've done. After my strategic reconnaissance, I climbed back down the ladder and entered the house.

67

The idea for the documents in the name of Agustín was accepted by everyone, and the girls wrote to their brother asking him to come.

Three days sufficed for my fever to go away. They were nights full of terrible dreams. Uncle Pepe was somewhat indiscreet. He wasn't afraid of anything. He had already contacted a Spaniard residing in Portugal who was a Republican and Freemason, attributes that had led him to be arrested and sent to Lisbon where he spent time in prison. There he met Spaniards and Portuguese who were enemies of Salazar's dictatorship. That is what Uncle Pepe told me. Thanks to the influence of his father-in-law, this Spaniard, whose name was Manolo Gómez, had been set free. When he was released, a Spanish chauffer who, by chance, was also named Manolo Gómez, was arrested in Portugal, taken to the Spanish border, driven to Ayamonte and shot without trial. The other Manolo Gómez, the one who had been released from jail, was married to a Portuguese woman whose father was an upstanding tax inspector, a member of Portugal's high society and a friend of the Salazar regime. For that reason, Manolo was very well-regarded by those in power. Uncle Pepe arranged an interview with him. We were to meet near a well on Almirante Reis Street, a hundred meters or so from the house as the crow flies.

I summoned all my courage, went out, and soon found myself with this gentleman. What a pleasant surprise! It was Manolo Gómez Sosa. We knew each other well. He had been a regular at our gatherings at the Republican Casino in Ayamonte. There was no need for introductions. We shook hands and Manolo initiated the conversation. He told me about his arrest and the fifteen days he spent in the Lisbon jail, during which time he feared being taken back to Spain. Fortunately for him, it had been his namesake, the chauffer, who was arrested and fell victim to the Fascist terror. As I listened, I was astonished by Manolo's cool composure.

I continue to be afraid and always on the alert. Manolo has told me not to worry about my economic situation. Uncle Pepe would receive a monthly payment for my expenses while my departure from Portugal was arranged.

"There is a magnificent solidarity between the enemies of the Portuguese dictatorship and Spanish Republicans. If the police here receive a document requesting your arrest, someone will come to warn you beforehand," he told me.

I am amazed. This interview has lifted my morale. My mistrust has diminished, but I am not out of the woods yet. At this point, we said good-by, arranging another interview for the following Sunday at the same time. I retraced my steps and entered the house, where I related everything Manolo Gómez Sosa had told me.

At my request, after we eat, I read aloud the items in the Portuguese newspaper to the cousins, who correct my pronunciation so I can begin perfecting my command of the language. Days go by with the hope of escaping from Portugal. My wish and goal was to make my way to the Spanish Republican zone and offer my services to the legitimate government. That was my dream. All my thoughts were focused on that idea. Meanwhile, I took care of the canaries.

One day, Uncle Pepe came back from work and sat down with me. "Tonight," he said, "they have arrested two boys from Galicia who were secretly working in a bakery, and have immediately taken them back to Spain. Don't be afraid. You are safe here. If anyone asks me, I will tell them you are my nephew Agustín, visiting us from Tavira."

I echoed his assurance of my security, but I did not trust it. In twenty-four hours, the panorama could change and I could be arrested, taken to the border, and my cadaver would appear in one of the Ayamonte squares to terrorize the residents. Always on the alert, in spite of the promises of Uncle Pepe and his friends, I thought about looking for another refuge in case this one was discovered.

That night while we ate, I told Uncle Pepe about my wish to seek safety somewhere else. We went out for a walk. Down by the well at the end of the street, we came to a store and went in. We were going to talk to a man who was there leaning on his elbows against the counter. He was compact and strong. When he turned to look at me, he hesitated a moment and then his eyes filled with joy. He was known as the bravest smuggler in the area. He knew how to cross the border wherever and whenever he wished. He was called José, 'The Pope,' and was quite well off, with farms in the countryside around Plixâo. It was this man, 'The Pope,' whom I had encountered during my first night as a fugitive.

He rushed toward me and gave me a hearty hug. He knew that I had crossed the river. He asked my family about me, but they had been unable to give him any information concerning my whereabouts. He told me, "If 'The Pope' couldn't find out where you were, the police wouldn't be able to find you either." But now he had found me and he was certain he could protect me.

"An hour after you crossed the river," he told me, "there was intense gunfire as they machine-gunned the boat you left adrift. When the border guards approached it, they found no one there, and surmised that the boatman was a smuggler who had fallen into the river. The customs guards' speedboat also came, and they were of the same opinion as the Portuguese guards."

Uncle Pepe was speechless. "You already know each other?" he said.

I briefly explained how I met 'The Pope' in a tavern called "The Sacristy" in Ayamonte and how, after a few drinks, we became fast friends. Then I told of my encounter with him on the night I escaped from town. We had a glass of wine and the three of us left the store together. I told 'The Pope' all about my situation and my wish to find another refuge in case the police came looking for me. 'The Pope' invited us to come with him. We were almost on the outskirts of town. I admired the courage and integrity of this man. He was a liberal, and as hostile to the dictatorial Portuguese regime as the police were to the regime's enemies.

As we walked, he said to me, "They are all against me because I have a son who, when he was born, I inscribed him in the Civil Registry with the name Lenin. My son is a student and his teachers have told me to have him baptized and change his name. Otherwise they won't pass him. And I told them that if they don't like my son, I will package him and ship him off to the Soviet Union. I also have a motorboat that I decided to name 'Parliament,' for which reason they have confiscated it."

The three of us kept on walking away from the town. I began to tell José Silva, which was the real name of 'The Pope,' how I had escaped from that hell. I told him, "Now that I know what they think happened to me, I am worried about what my family is going through."

"Don't worry. Tomorrow they will know you are safe and sound. And be assured that soon you will get a letter from them telling you how they are doing."

When we are well into the countryside, Uncle Pepe says he wants to return to the town but 'The Pope,' and I as well, want to get to his farm. After an hour of walking and talking, we arrived. It was a large house with its stables and all the trappings worthy of a successful farm. The door was open and inside, by the light of a kerosene lamp, there was a family shucking corn. 'The Pope' introduced me to the family: an old widow, a son, and a daughter. He explained the purpose of our visit, introducing me as a "fugitive" whom they would have to hide if I were being sought, so no one would know I was there.

We returned to the town, walking for an hour until we arrived in front of the house where 'The Pope' lived. He said good-by and told me, "Now I know where you live. I'll bring you news from Spain."

He gave me some coins, saying, "Here. This is for you to buy tobacco."

As we headed home, Uncle Pepe warned me: "Try not to be seen too often with this friend. Since he is a known smuggler and enemy of the regime, his house is closely watched and has been searched several times. Be careful not to fall into an ambush."

The First Letter

'The Pope' and all his friends had mobilized their resources on my behalf. It is a group composed of bus drivers, truckers, taxi drivers, shopkeepers, and boatmen, and has complicated interconnections that are difficult to explain. Night time, on both sides of the river, is their natural habitat. They signal to each other with lights, or by imitating the chirping of crickets or the croaking of frogs, and the meaning is understood on the other side of the river. Even the hooting of an owl serves to warn the others of danger. They pass enormous crates of eggs from Portugal to Spain, as well as hams and coffee, and from Spain to Portugal, they pass bolts of silk cloth and various spices, of which the most coveted is saffron.

Not twenty-four hours after my encounter with 'The Pope,' I received the first letter, delivered personally by him. I opened it with the emotion and anxiousness one could imagine. It was in my fiancée's handwriting: "We were tormented by the premonition that something bad had happened to you. Since you left, we haven't slept. There was the sound of gunfire on the river, and at dawn, my father went to the boat landing to find out if you had been arrested and brought back. Serafín was told that a smuggler had been attacked and had fallen into the water. No one mentioned your name. I see that with God's help, you will get through this difficult time. They say the killings are over but don't trust them. Get away as far as you can. They continue harassing us. Give your address to no one, absolutely no one."

How short the letter seemed to me. But I had to answer so the Fascists would know that I was no longer there and would leave my fiancée's family alone. I immediately checked in the newspaper, *Diario das Noticias*, for the list of ships that were about to embark from the Port of Lisbon for America. I wrote a letter to my brother, who was convalescing in the sanatorium in "El Parral," and told him that the following day I was boarding such and such ship destined for Mexico. The letter was dated in Lisbon. Then I wrote another, for one of Uncle Pepe's sisters who lived in Lisbon, asking her to stamp and mail the letter. Sure enough, the letter was mailed in Lisbon and arrived in Spain. Days later, 'The Pope' told me that the letter had arrived and was the cause of great happiness among my friends, as well as great surprise among my enemies. I was overjoyed by the impact caused by what I had written.

'The Pope' informed me that an individual who was a municipal guard in Ayamonte had escaped and was here in Olhâo. I was given the address where he was working. He was outside, sitting on a chair. I walked by him, passing very closely, and recognized him. Then, after continuing on a few meters, I turned and stood near him. He looked at me and rubbed his eyes in disbelief. The expression on his face was a mixture of confusion and fright. In fact, it was the guard, José González Barba, a member of our party. He looked around the deserted street, gave me a hearty embrace and again looked up and down the street. Then he asked me how I got out and where I was living. I explained everything that had happened to me, but did not tell him where I was living.

"What luck!" he said. "Now I am going to tell you about my odyssey. They went looking for me at my house, but I had already escaped. I walked at night, crossing more than a kilometer of marshland. I slept among the saltwater plants and had to defend myself every night from the rats that attacked me. I kept going until I reached the sea, where, with the help of a boatman to whom I promised a lot of money, I was able to cross the border. The thing is, I was born in Portugal and so, under the circumstances, I am Portuguese. That is what has saved me."

I was perplexed. We all thought he had Spanish nationality. "I have nothing to fear. I am in my country and can be of service to you in case you need it, but be careful. There is a woman here married to Aurelio 'El Tato.' She is from Ayamonte and knows you well and is a friend of the Fascists. Make sure she doesn't see you because she would report your presence. What do you intend to do?"

"Well," I responded, "I am looking for a way to get to the Republican zone."

"Don't worry. Just wait. They aren't killing anymore. Our time will come. We are going to shave the heads of the wives and children of those who have treated us so vilely, and parade them through the streets so they understand the crime of *lese humanité* they have committed."

It was almost midnight when I said good-by to him. I took the alleys through the darkest and least traveled parts of the town until I got to Uncle Pepe's house. I told them about my visit to Barba that night. Uncle Pepe listened and replied in an almost bitter tone, "If you want to get to a safe place, never again go out alone while you are in this house, or you will never get away. You can't defend yourself alone. When you step through this door, you do it with me and nothing will happen to you. I will know what I have to do."

An Honest Trade

Since I like to work and Uncle Pepe has a large number of birdcages, I keep myself busy taking care of his canaries. One day, so I could earn a little money without leaving the house, he proposed that I learn to build cages. I accepted the idea at once. That afternoon, he brought me wood, wire, carpentry supplies, and a drill with a fine bit. The paradoxes of destiny! I, who so cherished and yearned for freedom, was going to manufacture jails for the poor little birds.

In a few days, I constructed a model for the cages I would later mass-produce. Once the model was finished, I could build as many as three cages a day. On Sundays, Uncle Pepe took them to the closest town fair to sell them. In this way, I was able to earn enough to buy myself cloth for a suit. A tailor friend of the family came to the house to take my measurements. At his shop, he sewed the suit in the Portuguese style. With the new suit and a very Portuguese hat, all I needed was to master the language. To achieve that, every night while I twisted and cut wires, the cousins made me stop working and had me read a page from the newspaper, taking it upon themselves to correct my pronunciation. This method was so effective that in two months, I could pronounce Portuguese like a native.

Letters came almost every day, delivered to me in person. When they weren't from my fiancée, they were from some friend. I did not know who brought the letters nor did they know where I was hiding. It was 'The Pope' who received them. Then he would wait discreetly for Uncle Pepe to come out of the factory. After greeting him, he would walk a few meters with him and give him the letter surreptitiously so that no one would see.

Of all the letters, the longest and most emotional said: "Yesterday they brought the schoolteacher and former mayor of Ayamonte, Don Manuel Moreno Ocaña, from Río Tinto. For a whole day, they had him on public display, seated in a chair on Real Street, next to the hunting club. Then, surrounded by Falangists and guards, they paraded him through all the streets in town. They had hung a sign on his chest with the inscription, 'I am the mayor of the town.' When he passed the corner of the Falange headquarters, Rosa, Nene's daughter, insulted him, shouting, 'Now you are going to pay for what you've done.' We all saw it. Don Manuel's beard had grown out and his suffering was reflected in his face. He never bowed his head. He looked around at all the spectators as if begging some 'Simon the Cyrene' to emerge from among them to help him bear the ignominious cross. What bitterness must have filled his heart! We have learned that Frigolet, 'The Fat One,' who owns the tackle shop, spat at him and insulted him. Then they took the schoolteacher away, and it is not known where or when they killed him, much less where they buried him. . . ."

I was overcome by grief and my vision was blurred by tears. Poor Don Manuel Moreno Ocaña.[16] He was born in Torredonjimeno, a town in the province of Jaén, and came to work as a young teacher in Ayamonte, where he married the daughter of another teacher. The couple had four precious little daughters. He later became the first Socialist mayor of our town. From the time he arrived, he was the driving force behind the Socialist Party and taught classes for the workers so they could defend themselves from exploitation. For that reason, the leaders of the local oligarchy mounted a harsh campaign against him until the Minister of Public Instruction ordered his transfer to Salvochea, near Río Tinto. There, he continued his work for the Socialist Party in those mines. When the military coup was proclaimed, he joined the miners and, for several weeks, held out in this last pocket of Socialist resistance in the province of Huelva.

Sometimes I get to thinking about my situation. My anxiety grows. If I go out into the street, I risk being recognized by someone, which would inevitably lead to my being reported. Any person in a uniform terrifies me: a musician, a fireman—they all seemed to be coming to arrest me and I would avoid meeting them face to face. 'The Pope' tries to calm me, saying that the ones who could arrest me,

---

16 In Moreno Ocaña's dossier prepared by the Falange, on file in Salamanca, one reads: "Freemason, third degree. He belonged to the Redención Lodge, of Ayamonte, with the symbolic name 'Rousseau.' He took part as an orator in meetings held in the towns of the province before the Movement. There is no record of political antecedents" (11/27/1941). Manuel Moreno Ocaña, born 1894 in Torredonjimeno (Jaén), became a Freemason in 1924. In his Masonic file it states that in March 1932 his membership was cancelled for non-payment of dues and for failure to attend meetings. In 1953, fifteen years after his disappearance, the General Security Agency was still requesting his "Masonic Antecedents" from the National Delegation of Documentary Services, part of the executive branch of the government.

the Police for the Protection and Defense of the State, never wore uniforms. Generally, they came from Lisbon to carry out arrests when they were least expected. My nerves were in such a state that if someone knocked at the door, whether the milkman or the baker, I was instantly climbing the ladder to the roof terrace ready to take flight. Since I was continually talking about getting out of Portugal, 'The Pope' asked me if I knew how to sail. He told me there was a Portuguese native named José da Mónica who was in hiding because of his opposition to the Salazar dictatorship. He was planning to escape to Morocco in a small boat. Everything was to be carefully prepared down to the last detail. The prospect of this new adventure filled me with illusions. I could already see myself tending the jib sheet or taking turns at the tiller with José da Mónica.

After a few days went by, Uncle Pepe brought me the unpleasant news that José da Mónica had died. With the disappearance of this man, my hope of freedom vanished. There was another man who had a boat and made clandestine voyages taking refugees to Morocco. They called him 'O Amarelo,' 'The Yellow Man,' but, according to 'The Pope,' he was unscrupulous. After taking money from some of his prospective passengers, they were captured by the police at the moment of departure.

Days Go By

I continued making birdcages and waited for another opportunity to present itself. One day, Uncle Pepe's wife told me 'The Pope' was waiting for me in front of Bastos's store and that it was urgent I go see him. I went immediately and found him waiting for me, exactly where I'd been told he would be. We walked out into the countryside and, along the way, he gave me the news that some Falangists had come ashore at Villarreal and were headed this way to see if they could find me in the vicinity. Thinking I would be safer at his farm, 'The Pope' had come to get me as a preventive measure. We arrived at his farm. He gave me a broad-brimmed straw sombrero, a peasant's shirt, and a sickle.

Then he took me to a spot far from the house and told me, "Pretend you are harvesting this pea field. From here, you can keep an eye on the highway and the house. I am going back to town and will bring you news, tobacco, and whatever else you need."

Four days went by, during which I ate stone-ground corn flour cooked with water and salt. At night, only the barking of dogs could be heard. I slept upstairs in the house where there was a way to escape in the event of danger. On Sunday, 'The Pope' and Uncle Pepe showed up.

Poor Spanish Republic. Poor Spanish people who tried, for once, to have a say in the government. They are being killed, beaten, and condemned to silence. It seems as though, by the grace and works of God, power over the country had been conceded to the rich, the military, and the priests. But we can't give up. We would have to make a pact with the devil himself, if he exists, in order to defeat them. My hope is to get to the Republican zone to fight in our defense, and die if necessary.

Today, I am back in Olhâo, in the house of my friend from Ayamonte, Manolo Gómez Sosa, who lives here. He has invited me to his luxurious dining room to have a glass of cognac from our region. "The danger has passed," he told me. "Right there across from where you are sitting, Sulpicio, in his Falange uniform, was eating. Cuña's daughters and other women were here as well. They had come to see if they could find you because someone told them that a Spaniard was here walking about at will. They knew some details, which they had been told, but they couldn't find out much more. 'Little Pistol,' as they called you, 'must be around here somewhere,' they said. 'He sent a letter saying he was about to embark for Mexico, but we checked the passenger list and his name didn't appear on it.'

"I told them, 'That one is cleverer than you are. I am sure he has embarked under a false name. I know him well, just like I know his friend, the journalist Carlos Rivera.'

"'Carlos Rivera doesn't interest us. It's the other one we're after. He's going to get it but good when we catch him.'"

"Manolo, my friend," I replied, "I don't know why they see me as such a threat. Perhaps it is because I have published some articles in the newspapers and they are afraid I will accuse them for the murders they are committing. So many crimes, so many outrages and abuses. That is why they want to kill me, to eliminate an inopportune witness. I am proud of not having done anything to anyone. The whole town could verify that."

"If they catch you," said Manolo, "who would be able to come to your defense? If anyone tried, they would be killed along with you. They have already done it to others. Don't despair. We are already arranging a plan to send you to Lisbon. Once there, our friends will find a way for you to leave Portugal. You should notify your fiancée's relatives in the Portuguese capital so they can take you in with the greatest possible secrecy."

It was midnight when we left the house. Manolo accompanied me to the Rua da Liberdade, shaking my hand firmly three times when we said good-by.

The Incident

Uncle Pepe had a great love for canaries. He would spend his free time watching them, moving them from one cage to another, or arranging nests for their offspring. One day, he was at work in the factory. It was four in the afternoon and Aunt Luisa called me to stretch a piece of cloth for her to embroider. I left my workshop and entered the house. A few minutes later, we heard a noise in the patio. A cage with several canaries had fallen to the ground. It startled Aunt Luisa and me. I ran to the patio and saw that a canary with curly feathers that Uncle Pepe called a Belgian had died. The little birds used to peck at the wall, removing layers of whitewash around the nail that held up their cages and causing accidents like this one.

When Uncle Pepe came home from work and saw the dead canary, he became furious, insulting me with the crudest words I had ever heard, and threatening to report me to the police. "I am not your father. Go to your whore of a mother for protection." I watched him and headed for the door to seek out 'The Pope' and ask him to rescue me from this situation. Aunt Luisa, who saw the whole thing, prevented me from leaving, saying that Uncle Pepe's anger would quickly subside. By now, she knew his moods after so many years of marriage.

The next day, I saw 'The Pope' and told him what had happened. He went to see Manolo Gómez and asked him to put in motion a plan to get me out of Uncle Pepe's house. 'The Pope' called Uncle Pepe a fool who was taking advantage of my presence to charge an exorbitant amount for putting me up. Many months later, even after leaving Olhâo, I would become angry over that bitter moment when his words had stung my heart.

The following day, José da Silva, 'The Pope,' came to the house with a letter he had just received. The letter said: "They have called the families of those who had been killed to the town hall for them to sign a document stating that the deaths had occurred on the frontlines. In exchange, they would receive a small pension. Everyone signed except one woman who refused, declaring that it was a lie and that they themselves had killed her husband. It is also known that they killed our companions Próspero Álvarez, the mayor of Villablanca, and Matías, another Socialist and the mayor of Villanueva de los Castillejos.[17] It is said that they killed him with a short dagger in the back of the neck, as if he were some animal in a slaughterhouse. Now they are beginning to let many of the prisoners go, among them Antonio 'Bisera' who, during the massacres, became so

---

17 Próspero Álvarez Orta, the mayor of Villablanca, was killed in Huelva together with his brother Luis on August 10, 1936; Matías Rodríguez Márquez, the mayor of Villanueva de los Castillejos, met the same end two days earlier in the same city. Other mayors assassinated in the area were Juan Manuel Santana Suárez (Lepe), Alfonso Zunino Toscano (Cartaya), Rafael Zambrano Romero (Isla Cristina), and Miguel Rodríguez Ponche (La Redondela). The same fate would have befallen Manuel Flores Rodríguez, the mayor of Ayamonte, had he not escaped from the town on July 28 in the fishing boat "Guadiana." For a complete list of public officials eliminated in the province by the insurgents, see Francisco Espinosa Maestre, *La guerra civil en Huelva*, 397-408.

desperate, he tried to kill himself by running headfirst into the wall." Here the letter ended.

The river of blood in which Andalusian democracy and freedom was being drowned was greater than what the international press reported. Not a single small town or village escaped this well-organized crime. Townspeople lamented the great injustice being committed, because those beasts on the prowl had satiated themselves on poor citizens with humanitarian sentiments who were incapable of committing such acts. I remember when, a few days after the military coup, several well-armed militiamen from the mountains came to town in trucks with the intention of taking charge of the people who had been detained in the jail by government order. The Socialist mayor at the time, Manuel Flores Rodríguez, was vehemently opposed, declaring that the town of Ayamonte alone was responsible for the lives of those in its jail. The militiamen had to leave without accomplishing their aim. How different the town's Fascists were, denouncing their own neighbors and turning them over to the firing squads, sometimes because of personal grudges and sometimes because they wanted the dead man's job.

En Route to Lisbon

I arrived here with nothing and now I have a small suitcase with a change of underwear, a toothbrush and toothpaste, a case for my shaving needs, and everything required for a long journey. I said good-by to Aunt Luisa and the rest of the family and headed for a predetermined spot on the outskirts of town along the general highway. 'The Pope' was there, along with several of my Portuguese friends, to say good-by and wish me a good trip. Cousins María and Dolores had fastened a talisman, a small white horse made of marble, to my lapel so the person who would come looking for me would recognize me.

When night fell, a truck loaded with crates of fish and ice arrived. It was headed for the Lisbon fish market with its cargo. In the middle of the load, there was an empty spot where I was to travel. It was so small that my arms were squeezed against the crates. I laid my suitcase on the truck's floorboard and sat with my knees pressed against the crates in front of me. My back too was jammed against the crates behind me. Then they covered me from above with more fish crates. The truck started the journey at once.

The driver had told me that the truck's owner, who knew me, had given him the task of taking me as far as Lisbon and turning me over to a family member who would come looking for me. I could guess who the owner of the truck would be, Lieutenant Trindade, who had been forced into exile in Spain when the Portuguese dictatorship came to power. He had lived in our town and was called 'Redleg.' After many months in exile, he took advantage of a general amnesty and returned to Portugal. He never forgot all the things we had done for him. He was a close friend of Manolo Gómez.

I was getting cold. By then, we must have been approaching the famous police checkpoint in Caboço da Velha. Then I heard the driver say *"peixes, Lisboa"* [fish, Lisbon], and after a brief inspection, the truck was rolling again. It must have been about midnight. I breathed a deep sigh of relief at having gotten through that danger. My knees and hips began to hurt. My feet were in a pool of ice water and fish blood that splashed around my suitcase at every curve in the road. By two o'clock in the morning, the painful cold almost made me cry. My back was wet too. I wanted to sit up but I couldn't. It was a harsh trial I had to endure if I wanted to be saved. At four o'clock I tried to sleep, but to no avail. The truck stopped again. Another checkpoint. They asked for papers and the driver repeated the same words, *"peixes, Lisboa."* After ten endless minutes, the truck began to roll again, and some ten kilometers further on, I felt it leave the road. The motor stopped and the driver and his mechanic came in. They removed the crates that covered me and that had been dripping on me during the entire trip. The mechanic took one of my hands and the driver took the other and they lifted me up.

I tried to stifle the pain I was feeling at that moment in my knees and hips. They also took out my suitcase and laid me down in the grass. I asked them to rub me down with rum from the bottle I had in my suitcase, and they did. Gradually, my body began to warm up and the driver, as well as his mechanic, apologized for not having gotten me out sooner. During the night, they had had to stop at three checkpoints. Whenever they were driving away from one checkpoint, the trucks coming in the opposite direction signaled with their headlights to indicate the presence of another further up the road. That is why they couldn't take me out of there. My suitcase was soaked and I told them not to worry about it. My main concern was to get to Lisbon alive. I drank a few swigs of rum and so did the mechanic. The driver excused himself, saying he never drank when he was driving.

I was in the truck's cab between the driver and his mechanic when the sun came up. We were just a few kilometers from Lisbon. On this side of the River Tajo in a place called Cacilhas, they made me get out of the truck while they bought a ferry ticket for the truck and another for us. The driver maneuvered the truck onto the ferry, and the mechanic and I mingled with the scores of people heading to work in Lisbon across the Tajo. We disembarked in Lisbon, again staying close to the group of workers until the truck came ashore. First we went to the fish market, where there was a great din of fishmongers and buyers, women called *varinas*, who buy fish, wrap them in a type of plant fiber, and carry them on their heads, selling them door to door. While the truck was being unloaded, the driver brought a large glass of milk and a bread roll to the truck for me. I ate them with great delight.

It took more than an hour to unload and sell the fish. We left the market and went to a small plaza where the stores' metal shutters were still closed. A short man with glasses and a briefcase appeared and the driver ordered me out of the truck. The man approached and shook our hands, looking at the small marble horse on my lapel. He smiled and said, "This is the one."

Then the driver handed me a small bag with money in it and said, "This is the collection taken up by your friends the day you left."

It was about seven o'clock in the morning as we crossed a number of streets, leaving the truck far behind, along with those good Portuguese friends who had brought me this far. I couldn't thank them enough for their humanitarian act. "I am Uncle Joaquín Campos. I am married to Encarnación González, first cousin of your fiancée's father. I have two daughters and two sons. You will be safe in my house."

We got to an avenue where we boarded a streetcar that took us a long way. "This is the Poço do Bispo neighborhood where the Braço de Prata arms factory is located. We get off here," he said. "And this is where we live, the first apartment to the left."

The New Family

They have received me with open arms. Aunt Encarnación gave me a hug. Cousin Joaquín looked to be about twenty years old and Cousin Hilda, eighteen. The other two were Marciana, twenty-five years old and single, who worked in the cigarette factory, and Pedro, the oldest, who was married. He and his wife both worked. The building where we lived was called Predio Santos Lima and had been a refuge for Lisbon's anarcho-syndicalists. It was machine-gunned at the beginning of the dictatorship. I have given a brief account of my entire odyssey, especially the uncomfortable night I spent between Olhâo and Lisbon. I asked them to put my little suitcase, which had more papers in it than clothing, out in the sun to dry, and I also asked for a little corner where I could sleep a few hours. They made me another cup of coffee with milk and put me in a small but comfortable bed. I slept almost until one. When I awoke, the family was eating. Uncle Joaquín, who worked at the unemployment office, had arrived and so had cousin Marciana.

I got up and found a pair of pants and a shirt on the chair. They weren't mine. They had been put there for me because my clothing was full of sea salt and the liquids that had dripped from the fish crates. I washed, combed my hair, and went out to greet my new family. There was already a place set for me at the table. They invited me to sit down and I apologized for my appearance. We were eating when there was a knock at the door. Cousin Hilda came in saying, "There is a gentleman asking for Miguel."

Needless to say, I jumped up and was preparing to rush out and climb over a neighbor's fence. Aunt Encarnación stopped me, saying that her husband had checked and seen that it was a friend "of our stripe" from Olhâo, who had been told that I was staying here and came to greet me and offer to help in any way he could. They had just phoned him and he had come at the urging of Lieutenant Trindade. Uncle Joaquín came in, and when he described the man to me, I went out to invite that gentleman in. We sat down on a sofa in the living room. I recognized him when I saw him because, naturally, we had met once in Olhâo when I was with Manolo Gómez. His name was Israel Isaac and he worked as a sales representative for an American film company. His job took him all around Portugal from town to town, which provided him the opportunity to distribute clandestine copies of *Avante*, a newspaper opposed to the dictatorship. After only a few minutes of conversation, he assured me that he would get me out of Portugal en route to a free country. He gave me an envelope containing some money and a card with his address.

Then he went on to say, "Things are not going well. This is going to trigger a world war. The Germans have the best arms in Europe and they are calling for the triumph of the insurgent generals. The French and English are afraid of getting involved in a war over Spain. Portugal has a bilateral alliance with England, but Salazar sees the writing on the wall and is distancing himself from the British and making overtures to Germany. That is why he is helping Fascist Spain."

"What about Russia?" I said. "Where is the friendship with workers who are falling by the dozen?"

"Russia," he replied, "is an unknown factor and is too far away. It will not intervene the way the Germans and Italians are. Russia encourages internal revolutions in other countries and provides economic aid in order to establish governments that support its policies. Sometimes it sends technicians. That is all Russia does. I want to make it clear that I am not a Communist, but to fight against the dictatorship we have here, I would ally myself with the devil himself if he exists."

Since my conversation with him was in perfect Portuguese, he said, "I am amazed how well you pronounce our language. You can go out wherever you like. No one will suspect you are Spanish. You already have my address. If any difficulty arises, phone me or pay me a visit." When we said good-by, he said, "I want you to know that it is not the Portuguese people who oppose the Spanish Republic. It is our government and its lackeys." Uncle Joaquín took advantage of the opportunity to ask if he could find a job for cousin Joaquín. Israel promised to look into it.

"What a courageous fellow," I said to myself.

Uncle Joaquín went with him to the hallway. I have returned to the dining room. Everyone had already eaten, leaving my share and that of Uncle Joaquín. I was feeling fairly confident, especially living in a city like Lisbon where people don't know each other.

My back feels cold. Marciana and Uncle Joaquín have gone back to their jobs and Aunt Encarnación sends me back to bed. I close my eyes and dream that my hands are clutching oars. In the darkness, I see Zambujera Hill on the shore of the River Guadiana. At dawn, Uncle Joaquín came into the room. He put his hand on my forehead and said I had a fever. He brought an aspirin and a glass of herbal tea with rum. "Drink this and stay in bed. You'll feel better tomorrow."

I Pay My Friend a Visit

I went out unaccompanied and headed toward downtown Lisbon, taking one streetcar after another and summoning all my courage. Sometimes I glanced sidelong at anyone who could be a policeman. Everything went well and, with help from no one, I arrived at the office where Señor Israel worked. There were many employees there who were watching me, but they never even suspected who I was. He received me with considerable pleasure.

The first thing he asked me was whether I had his address, to which I answered in the affirmative. "Well tear it up. Now you know where to find me for anything you might need. Addresses in a pocket are evidence for an accusation."

I took out the paper and shredded it with my fingers. My friend smiled. He invited me to visit him the following Sunday at his house in Cintra up in the mountains. He gave me all kinds of details: what train to catch, where to get off, and the street and number of his chalet. I told him that the object of my visit was to find the Mexican representative to Portugal.

"The Mexican Legation is a little further up the street. But be careful because it is closely watched. Take this big briefcase so you will look like one of the employees or a courier. On Sunday, you can tell me the outcome of your visit."

I headed out into the street. With my Portuguese suit, my sombrero with its curled brim, and the large briefcase, I am afraid of nothing. It was a defect of mine. When I get an idea into my head, I am relentless in its pursuit. I got to the avenue where the Mexican Legation was located, in a first floor office. From the corner, I saw there were two men with the kind of hats plainclothesmen would wear and said to myself, "There they are." I waited until a group of people were going by and slipped into their midst. It's possible they can't help me with my problem here. I am living undercover in an enemy country that has no respect for international laws regarding the right to asylum. I have already seen plenty of evidence for that. If I am unlucky enough to be arrested by the police, I will be immediately taken to the border, and I have seen how those who are handed over there are killed without any legal proceedings.

The group of people I am with has arrived at the Mexican Legation. I entered the corridor without being seen. The door was open and when I knocked on it a few times, a boy came out. I asked him to tell the Mexican representative I needed to see him. The boy took me into an office where a young gentleman asked me the object of my visit. In a few words, I described my odyssey.

He listened to me in silence and said, "You must have a lot of balls to have gotten this far."

And I said, "Nothing of the sort. It is fear, terror, which has sent me running here." Then he offered me a cigarette and, while we smoked, I told him about my wish to find a way to the Republican zone.

He said, "I am very sorry, but we can't do anything directly. I am going to be perfectly honest with you. Because of the war in Spain, we don't have very good relations with the Portuguese government. Consequently, we have to do what we can to contact the English and French representatives. They have commercial interests here and are respected. Meanwhile, give me your address and some way of notifying you just in case."

I understood the whole situation, the whole truth of this gentleman's words. He left and returned with several packets of magnificent cigarettes from the "El Águila" factory in Mexico. He said good-by with genuine warmth, apologizing for not being able to provide the protection I needed. "Be careful as you leave. Keep your eyes open."

I put the packets of cigarettes in the big briefcase and went out to the hallway near the entrance. I looked out into the street and saw how a man in a plainclothes-style hat was strolling along near the corner. A group of men and women were coming up the street and I slipped in among them. I had not been seen either entering or leaving. With the briefcase under my arm, I passed street after street until I got to the Plaza del Rosío in central Lisbon, hub for the streetcars to the various neighborhoods. I boarded the one for Poço do Bispo and arrived home while the family was eating. I told them about my visits and how I had spent the morning. I showed my packets of Mexican cigarettes and Uncle Joaquín congratulated me on my courage and stealth, moving about the city like that.

More News

This letter that I have just received had three envelopes. I suppose the first, which is blank, was passed by hand across the border at Villarreal. In that town, they put it in another envelope that was addressed to Uncle Pepe's house in Olhâo. In Olhâo, the cousins put it in a third envelope and sent it to Aunt Encarnación's house, and here it is in my hands. It was written by my fiancée. I am reading it and it says, "We are writing you today to wish you health and good luck. While these people celebrate their triumphs at the front, we and our friends feel like crying. Some of them, it seems, are beginning to realize that what they've done is insane. Some of them are still here. Others have left. There are also some who have suffered God's punishment, for example, Duarte the corporal, who has had a stroke which has completely paralyzed his right hand, the one he used when beating our companions. The 'Pachanitos,' who were accused of painting the word 'Murderers' on the walls, have been taken to the border because they are Portuguese. José, Chanoca's son, has been released from jail thanks to a good-conduct certificate given to him by his employer, Cipriano Carrasco. The whereabouts of Sebastián, president of the Socialist Youth movement, is still unknown. If he is caught, his name will be added to the list of the fallen, just like Eliseo. Don't worry about him because they won't find him. Everything is in short supply here. There is no fabric or bread or cigarette papers or anything. Whoever has a friend who is a smuggler makes do buying on the black market. Nene's daughter, who unleashed her wicked tongue against us, especially the day they paraded the schoolteacher and former mayor Don Manuel through the streets, began to have hallucinations and spent her nights in a state of panic. One day, she threw herself into the cistern that was in her house and drowned. They had to use tuna hooks to get her out. The saddest news for you is that your brother Pepe died in the Huelva hospital, and your brother Paco was forced to enlist in a Carlist militia, 'Requetés del Rocío.' I have enclosed a photograph of you that a girl from Carmen Street gave me."

This letter has left me saddened by the death of my brother. I examined my photograph, taken on May 1, 1936, the day of the workers. I was wearing a red silk shirt. On the back of the photograph, they had written, "May God save you, Miguel." The inscription was in keeping with the letter and its description of Duarte's stroke. He was an informer and agent of the Fascists who had carried so many of our companions off to their deaths. With that arm hanging limply while his fellow Fascists saluted in celebration of their victories at the front, he was paying for his crimes. Meawhile, she of the "wicked tongue," also known as 'Vespers,' had taken justice into her own hands, punishing herself for her evil deeds.

Journalistic Lies

In this house where I am being sheltered, one can hear the rapid fire of the machine guns being repaired at the nearby arms factory in Braço de Prata. I know that trucks come to pick up loads of materiel for Spain. The drivers are the sons of the "wealthy gentlemen" of our unhappy nation, and so are the mechanics. It is the best way to keep them from going to the frontlines. There is a small group of Portuguese activists who have already blown up the gunpowder factory in Marvila, as well as a truck full of munitions near the Spanish border. But this is not enough to make the world aware of Portugal's flagrant intervention on behalf of those insurgents who rebelled against Spain's legitimate government. I have heard irrefutable reports of how they handed over the Socialist parliamentary deputy, Don Nicolás de Pablo, on the Badajoz border. He was executed in a public square in the capital of that Extremaduran province.

In reference to this incident, I read in the Portuguese newspapers the monstrous lie of Portugal's representative to the Non-Intervention Committee, Armindo Monteiro, who declared, "Don Nicolás de Pablo has not been in Portugal. If he entered clandestinely, he must have returned again by the same procedure."[18] In the wake of the fall of Badajoz, hundreds of people fled to various points along the Portuguese border, which many of them managed to cross, among them Nicolás de Pablo. Portuguese police arrived by night with buses and told the fugitives they would take them to Lisbon. The buses headed that way for several hours before taking another highway that returned to Badajoz. Some of the fugitives who noticed the change of direction jumped from the vehicles and continued toward Lisbon on foot. Some were hunted down. Others blended in like I had and found someone to protect them until they could find a way out of Portugal. I had contacts with one who had found work in a floor tile factory. He made good money. The owner of the factory was a friend of the Spanish Republic.

There was an order from the police that was published in the newspapers. All of the doormen, cleaning women, and apartment managers had to send the names of everyone living in their building to the nearest police station, whether it was a new tenant living alone or someone who had moved in with one of the families residing there. This order meant that even the cleaning women were obliged to help the police in their search for Spanish refugees. In general, no one dared commit such an atrocious injustice.

---

[18] The Socialist deputy Nicolás de Pablo was turned over by the Portuguese government to the Fascist authorities of Badajoz together with, among others, the mayor of Badajoz, Sinforiano Madroñero, a few days after the occupation of that Extremaduran city. In fact, he was assassinated during the last days of August 1936 in a public square. A band had been hired to play music for the occasion. His death was never recorded in any Civil Registry.

Dutch coal ships were providing an enormous service. Their crews carried out the risky mission of hiding some of the fugitives who were in danger and evacuating them from Portugal. Also involved was a well-organized group of Portuguese citizens who worked to find and protect undocumented Spaniards and get them aboard those vessels. The evacuated fugitives carried letters addressed to Señor Álvarez del Vayo and Don Luis Jiménez de Asúa, the representatives of Republican Spain on the Non-Intervention Committee. The letters contained detailed accounts of all that was going on in Portugal.

The days pass quickly and the Portuguese newspapers celebrate the victories of the "rebels," who are embarked on a crusade in which the German role is revealed to the world when their warships bombard the Almería highway. The collaboration of Fascist Italy is also revealed as they patrol the entire Mediterranean, cutting off all possibility of Russian aid to the Republic. Meanwhile, the young men of Spain are being decimated and, in the forests of Andalusia, nothing remains in the moonlight but hundreds of mass graves with the anonymous corpses of those who have fallen to this scourge, which is unequalled since Attila's horse ravaged the earth.

In Cintra

I promised I would go to the house of that good gentleman who was protecting me. This mountain village was more like a residential town of individual chalets which housed only people of high political or industrial importance. This is where Don Alejandro Lerroux and Don José María Gil Robles were living.[19] From this ringside seat, they are cheering on the matadors in the bullfight that is taking place across the border in Spain.

I was in the Central Lisbon station very early, with my face buried in the sports page of a newspaper. There was a continual coming and going of people at that moment. I bought my ticket and approached the platform from which my train to Cintra would depart. I turned the brim of my hat lower and lower, discreetly observing the people passing by, fearful that at any instant, one of them might come and ask for my documents. It was possible that someone might recognize me and I was impatient to leave. Finally

---
19 Gil Robles was very busy in Portugal. We know, for example, that a few days after the occupation of Badajoz, he was active in the arms trade, serving as intermediary between the Badajoz Falange and certain Portuguese agents. See Francisco Espinosa Maestre, *La justicia de Queipo: Violencia selectiva y terror fascista en la II División en 1936* (Córdoba: Gráficas Mvnda, 2000), 185.

the train arrived and I boarded it, found a seat, and opened my newspaper, almost covering my face. An inopportune traveler next to me has struck up a conversation. We talked about sports. At one point, this passenger asked me, "Have you ever been to South America?"

"Why do you ask?" I responded.

"Because there is a certain lilt in your accent as if you were from Argentina or around there."

"You have guessed it," I said, "that is where I am from. I was born there of Portuguese parents."

"And are there many Portuguese there?" he asked.

I tried to indulge him with an invented statistic that seemed to satisfy him, and I gave him a fabulous description of the Pampa with its pastures and its innumerable cattle.

"Are you going to Cintra?" he asked. I responded affirmatively.

"Do you have family in Cintra?" he insisted. His question froze me in my tracks because I did not want to compromise anyone.

"No, I don't have family there. I am going to see a friend of my family."

"Do you mind telling me who the gentleman is?" he asked.

"I have the address in my briefcase. I will give it to you after we arrive," I told him.

I was having a bitter time of it and did not know how to get rid of that importunate traveler who was causing me so much suspicion and fear. When we arrived at the Cintra station, my friend was waiting for me. He saw me get off the train, followed by the other traveler, and approached me smiling. Before I could say anything, my traveling companion intervened, shaking my friend's hand and announcing, "Señor Isaac, here is your friend from Argentina."

Isaac smiled and said to me, "It's alright, it's alright. Don't be concerned. This gentleman is as much your friend as I am. He is one of us."

I was in Cintra for a few days, fishing in the Colares, a river that cascaded down the mountains. From a distance, I saw Don Alejandro Lerroux, leader of the Radical Party and an anticlerical revolutionary in his youth, who, once in power, put the brakes on all the impetus of his combative life and joined forces with the reactionary elements, thereby sowing disorder and provoking the present war. The other exile in residence was José María Gil Robles, the formidable church lawyer who threw so many obstacles in the path of the Republic. Both were here waiting for the Spanish windstorm to subside. It would have been better if they had remained in Spain after all their efforts to trip up the government and after all the laws they had torpedoed, practically annulling the work of parliament. Don Alejandro had incited the people to revolution on several occasions, and when that revolution finally occurred, he panicked and tried to crush it. Without doubt, he would sell his soul to the devil in order to die in peace, now that he is old and has lost all his combative spirit.

The Meeting in Cintra

One night, Señor Israel invited me to come with him. We entered what could be called the back room of a shop. It was fairly large and there were about twenty people there, only one of them familiar to me, my companion from the train. I greeted and shook hands with all of them, one by one. A tall gentleman with glasses, who was called 'The Professor,' got up and began to speak about the war in Spain. After a few minutes, he turned to me and said, "We would like to clarify whether it is true or not that the Spanish Republic was going to create the Union of Iberian Socialist Republics with the annexation of Portugal, which would thereby cease to be a free and independent nation."

I replied that that information was completely false, just like the death lists the Fascists had "discovered" in each city hall and which served to justify the liquidation of those they considered enemies. "The military insurgents have the three essential things they need: arms, foreign support, and lies. They claim to be leading an anti-Communist crusade, which is absurd because there had only been four Communist deputies in the parliament. Their only aim is to end democracy. Germany and Italy want to extend their economic control over Europe, especially in Spain, and to displace France and England from the markets they intend to conquer, including even the occupation of North Africa. It is for these reasons they have armed and trained the Spanish military rebels. France and England have put more of their trust in treaties than in the standards of international law, but treaties are no defense in the face of military aggression. By now, they have realized that this will lead to a world war. Republican Spain has never had, nor does it now have, any interest in annexing Portugal, whose inhabitants are zealous about their independence and want to preserve the heritage of their forbearers, which is the Portuguese colonial empire. If there has been disagreement and friction between the governments of our two countries, it has been because the Spanish Republic is a democracy and because, with its respect for international law, it has tried to protect and has protected Portuguese political refugees pursued by the Salazar dictatorship who have gone to Spain where they enjoy the right of asylum. In Portugal, there have been nuclei of anti-Republican Spaniards, military men, and powerful men of wealth, who have helped forge the most frightful disorder that Spain has ever known. Everything being said about the absorption of your country is a lie. The Generalitat of Catalonia and the Basque government, increasingly autonomous during the Republic, can vouch for that."

I spoke for over an hour, and they listened without interrupting me. I had clarified many things they wanted to know. There were functionaries there from various ministries and it was urgent for me to gain their confidence in order to get out of Portugal, which was my primary objective.

"What facility you have for expressing yourself in Portuguese. You now have more people who support you," my friend told me. I left the back room at the urging of Señor Israel, while he remained to talk to the others. When he came out, he told me we could go.

That night at my friend's house, I slept the way I used to. His wife was from Ceuta in Spanish Morocco and spoke correct Spanish. They woke me up early. I have washed and had breakfast, and half an hour later, a gentleman with a luxurious automobile arrived. I said good-by to Señor Israel's entire family and got into the car next to the chauffer, who gave me an envelope with money.

"Good luck, young man," he said to me when we arrived at my house. Only Aunt Encarnación and Cousin Hilda were home. The others were at work, even little Joaquín, who, thanks to the intervention of Señor Israel, was employed in a rubber factory in Marvila. I recounted my adventures to the family. They were all at ease. I was the one who distrusted everybody. Two days later, the chauffer of the luxurious car returned and left a voluminous bundle for me. It contained a navy blue overcoat, leather gloves, underwear, and a pair of shoes.

Departure

It was on April 11, 1939, when they came for me.[20] It was three o'clock in the afternoon. Aunt Encarnación and Hilda were full of emotion. It was the last time I was going to play the dangerous card of escape. I prepared my little suitcase with all the clothing and papers I had. More papers than clothing. I hugged each member of the family and, with my suitcase in hand, I descended the stairway of the famous Predio Santos Lima building. My heart skipped a beat. There were two people in the car and I was afraid it was a trap. They handed me a document which would serve as a safe-conduct pass. It contained my photograph. I read it as I stood there, before entering the car. It said, "We of the French Consulate in Lisbon request that all civil and military authorities grant safe passage to Miguel Domínguez Soler, native of Ayamonte, of Spanish nationality, office worker, and further request they grant him succor and protection in case of necessity." Then came the date and, on the back, the seal of the Police for the Protection and Defense of the State with the following comment: "Approved

---
20 This was ten days after the unconditional surrender of the Spanish Republic to the forces of Franco.

for embarkation on the ship 'Aurygni,' April 11, 1939." My cards were on the table and there was no other way out but to play them.

We arrived at the Port and they parked the car near the gangway of that majestic vessel. The chauffer gave me the following instructions: "When I give you the signal, climb the gangway as fast as you can. All the other passengers are already on board. At the top of the gangway, there is a table with an official known as the 'interviewer.' On each side of him, there are policemen who should not take your document before the interviewer. They are going to raise the gangway at four o'clock, ten minutes from now. Get ready." I received the order with extraordinary peace of mind. "Now," they told me. I didn't even have time to say good-by. With my suitcase in hand, I ran up the gangway and handed my paper to the interviewer. My heart was pounding furiously.

One of the policemen asked for the paper and read it, after which he turned to me and said, "Where are you going?"

"To Mexico," I responded.

"Who put you up during your stay in Portugal?"

"I have worked wherever I could," I stammered.

"You, what you should do is go to your town's cemetery."

"I haven't committed murder or robbery, nor have I harmed anyone."

"Look how well the son of a bitch speaks Portuguese," the other policeman said.

The interviewer stood up and, seeing me unable to hold back my tears, grabbed the paper from the hands of the policeman and told them, "This gentleman is presently on French soil and under my protection. Here is the seal of your superiors and the corresponding signature granting him permission to board this vessel. Do me the favor of leaving at once. I am about to raise the gangway."

He quickly grabbed me by the arm and led me inside the ship. "And you. Why are you crying? You are crying like a little girl. Come on. Let's go have a beer while your fright subsides," he said to console me. And he added, "The French Consulate had already phoned me to ask me to receive you and not to raise the gangway until you arrived. Now rest. There are real friends waiting for you in Casablanca. Have a drink to celebrate your freedom and your return to the world."

The interviewer was Spanish, of Basque origin. He was already working on the ship when he received the news of the military coup, and he used to tremble with fear each time they put into a Spanish port. "You've been lucky," he told me.

I have a cabin all to myself. I left my little suitcase and went out to watch the vessel leave the dock. This is the beginning of the freedom I so yearned for, the freedom I had so often dreamed about and for which I had suffered so much, and it is the French consul and a French ship that have saved me. I think of how appropriate it is that French land is burying these Spanish conflicts. In France are buried the kings, dictators, and Republicans who couldn't live side by side in their own country.

I take a stroll to explore the large vessel. Huge sleeping quarters with beds stacked on both sides. Down the middle is a corridor where there was a great movement of passengers, most of them Portuguese emigrants and a great number of girls between sixteen and twenty-five years old who, fleeing from Hitler, had been protected by an international organization called HILSEN. They were going to Brazil. There were also Nordic and German Jews who were fleeing from the possibility of an imminent European war.

Since I had occasion to run into my friends, Inés and Acevedo 'The English,' while I was in Lisbon, my multi-lingual conversations with them now enabled me to make my way in this intricate jungle of languages and become acquainted with one of those beautiful blond girls. It was she who greeted me first, with a "*bonjour*," and I responded in kind. We struck up a conversation. She had been educated at a prestigious academy in Warsaw and explained the odyssey she was embarked upon. All the girls belonged to liberal and anti-Fascist families. We sat down on one of the benches on the deck and soon we found ourselves surrounded by girls, who observed me as if I were some strange being. She soon asked, "Who are you?" And so, I too explained my odyssey, starting with my escape across the River Guadiana from the consequences of the terrible military coup that was to leave such a mark on the nation's life. As I spoke, my little friend translated what I said into Polish. Some of the girls were staring at me as if I were some poor devil in a novel that had become reality.

My translator's name was Irena. Since the girls were on their way to Brazil, they asked me how to say hello in Brazil and, knowing Portuguese, I told them. One of them, the oldest as far as I could tell, brought a notebook and wrote down the words. So I soon found myself with a chorus of more than a hundred studious girls who wanted to learn the language of the country where they were headed. I enjoyed my role as an accidental professor. The bell rang, announcing that the dining hall was open. Irena dismissed the class and told the students something I didn't understand. She took my hand and led me to the dining hall, saying, "I'm not going to let you go. After we eat we must resume our study of Portuguese."

When dinner was over, I let myself be led by the group of strong, blond girls. How relieved their parents must be to see them out of harm's way! They take me up on deck and make me sit under a light, Irena to my right and two other girls to my left, each with their respective notebooks.

We are sailing the Atlantic in the middle of spring. It dawns on me that I am truly free and I feel the urge to shout out, "*Viva la libertad!*" Everything I have been through seems as if I had watched it in a movie.

Irena would ask me questions in French and I would translate the question and the answer into Portuguese. They are putting together a Polish-Portuguese dictionary. It will serve them well in Brazil. I am not tired. We are all enjoying ourselves. It is the happiness of youth and also the blend of races and religions in search of a new life and new horizons. According to my watch, it is twelve-thirty at night. We need to rest. Tomorrow will be another day.

One of the girls has protested, "Why tomorrow? We must do it all today. Tomorrow, Señor Miguel will leave us and the classes will be over."

"Give us your address and we will write to you," said Irena.

"Tell them I am homeless, with neither a house nor a country of my own. Maybe one day, the survivors of this catastrophe, of this universal insanity, will meet again and celebrate the triumph of all that is humane and beneficial to everyone." I got up and went straight to my cabin. A cabin all to myself. A recompense for my sacrifices, provided by my Portuguese friends, whom I will never forget.

The "Aurygni," escorted by dolphins, was slipping through the calm waters with a slight pitching motion. I have learned that all the girls had been through a dreadful time because of a windstorm they weathered off northern Spain. They had all been nauseous, some of them terribly sick. By now, they have their sea legs. That is why they were laughing. They were waiting for me to be seasick. It was my turn. Irena let them know that I was born on the coast or, as I explained to them, with one foot on land and the other in the sea.

Thinking about my life, with its unexpected turns, I closed my eyes and dropped off into a profound sleep.

En Route to Casablanca

With the sun already up and its light streaming through the round portholes into my cabin, I felt a tickling sensation on my lips. It was Irena, who had come to say good morning. She was kissing me. Her blue eyes, like those of a young cat, made me tremble with emotion. I scarcely had time to envelope her in my bare arms. And then...

"Today you are leaving us. How little time we have had together! Tonight you will sleep in Casablanca and by a cruel and fateful destiny we will never see each other again," she said.

One after another, the other young girls came into my cabin. Irena, nervous and almost shouting, ordered them to leave so I could get up. There was laughter, unabashed laughter. It was Irena who was the first to leave. Eventually the others followed her, but the joking didn't stop there. Some of them, before they left, threw themselves on my bed, tickling me.

Back to the "*école*," as Irena called it. That day, even more pupils crowded around. Just like the previous evening and night, the lesson proceeded according to each girl's questions. The answers were in Portuguese and Irena told me that she was a little tired. The two of us got up as the rest of the group protested.

While we were strolling along the deck, the "interviewer" came by and told me, "You have had a formidable success on this ship. You are known to everyone. Get your things together, because this afternoon you will have to disembark in Casablanca."

I am overcome by sadness. Into the unknown once again. What will my life be like in this foreign land? Some of the girls take pictures of me, sometimes alone and sometimes in groups.

"Come with us to Brazil," Irena said to me.

"I can't. I don't know anyone there. I don't know anyone here either, but I have the consolation that Spain is not far away, and I am hoping that, when freedom rings again for my country, I will be nearby."

I gathered my things and climbed to the deck with my suitcase. The Port of Casablanca is already at our bow. I check my pocket for my safe-conduct pass. There were some affectionate embraces I will never forget and some tears and, once the gangway was lowered, I disembarked.

From below, I saw the ship's railing crowded by the girls cheering for me and waving to me. I approached the international police of the Port of Casablanca and presented my safe-conduct. The officer read it, saluted me, and shook my hand. Then he invited me into his office, telling me in correct Spanish, "Wait here a few minutes while I verify the other passengers. I want to talk to you."

I did as he told me. When he had completed the verification, the officer, whose name was Señor López, returned and said, "You are now among friends and in a free country. Do you have family or acquaintances in Casablanca?"

"I don't know anyone. I know that some friends from my area live in Casablanca, but I don't have their addresses."

"Don't worry," he said, "we will find them soon enough. One more thing, your document says you are an office worker, but you won't be able to find that kind of work here. Is there anything else you can do to earn a living?"

"Yes," I replied, "I know how to can sardines."

"Are you sure?"

"Yes, sir. Take me to a canning factory and I will show you."

"We'll see if you're telling the truth."

The police officer called to a small boy and told him to take me to the hotel "Les Amis," which was located at the entrance to the Medina. The room was on the first floor and smelled of cockroaches. I sat on the bed and read the name of the café where I was supposed to go the next morning, "Le Glacier," on the other side of the "Plaza de Francia." I went out for a walk, staying close to the hotel so I wouldn't get lost. There were many stores where you could buy anything, from roasted meats to vegetables, fried fish, bread, liqueurs. I asked where I could buy stationary, postcards, and stamps, and discovered that everyone spoke Spanish. In a few minutes, I was at a post office buying everything I needed. I went back to the hotel and spent hours writing to my fiancée and all of my friends in Spain and Portugal. Then I went out and had a light meal at one of the many cod shops in the neighborhood.

I slept well, with no fear or danger, and at seven o'clock I was shaving and ready to go to my meeting in the café "Le Glacier," where I was to be introduced to people who could help me. This café was located right in the center of Casablanca, at the end of the "Boulevard de Lagare," and it even had a kind of stage where artists who sang and danced sevillanas performed every night. It was the meeting place for the "intellectuals" of Spanish "refugeeland." I ordered coffee with milk and a large slice of buttered toast. Here the owners, the waiters, and almost all the clients speak Spanish. This cheers me up considerably. It seemed as if my life had just changed one hundred percent. Señor López, the police officer, arrived and asked if I had had breakfast yet. I answered affirmatively.

"I have a job for you," he said. "This morning, you will come with me to see a canning factory that is closed because the technician is ill."

"I need to earn enough to take control of my life," I responded.

"One of your people has just come in," he informed me and called out, "Don Pablo."

I turned my head and to my great surprise, I found myself face to face with my compatriot Don Pablo Ojeda Ojeda, who had been president of the Provincial Government of Huelva, and who saved his life when he escaped in a boat from Ayamonte on the night of July 29, 1936. In the blink of an eye, I was on my feet and embracing him. What an emotional moment!

"Little Miguel," he said, "when we heard about the killings in our town, we said that you must have been among the first to fall. Tell me, tell me everything. Don't leave out a single detail."

Another of my friends arrived, Antonio Mateo, who used to work with me at the provincial hospice, which was run by the Huelva government. It was the moment of a reunion I had dreamed about. My story took more than an hour. Don Pablo, who was one of the driving forces in the Masonic Lodge, listened with great emotion as I described the assault on the Lodge, the humiliating deaths of some of its members, and the tragedy of the schoolteacher Don Manuel Moreno, who also belonged to the Lodge. Then, it was my turn to listen. Antonio Mateo's story seemed as if it had been taken from a crime novel. Later, I would take him with me to see if I could find him a job at the Algero-Marocain canning factory, which was closed because the technician who ran it was hospitalized, apparently with cancer.

"But man," Don Pablo said, "here there are hundreds of refugees who need work. I have no idea how they get by. Let's see if you get lucky."

"Later, perhaps within an hour, I will be back."

I left with Señor López, who drove me in his automobile to the factory, which was in Roches-Noires, a working-class neighborhood in Casablanca. It was a rather small factory for my ambitions. I was received there by the owner, Monsieur Duchateau, who took me around to see the pressure cookers, the preparation tables, the brine vats, and the canning machines.

Since my mother had suckled me in a cannery, there was nothing in these places I was not familiar with. And then there were the daily conversations about the problems that arise in the preservation of fish. If I had been born in Jabugo, I think I would have been an expert in the manufacture of cured hams, because I have always been interested when the manufacture and sale of foodstuffs is being discussed. I could see that the factory was ready to operate even though, if I had had the time, I would have made some changes.

I immediately announced, "Everything is in order. Send a worker to prepare the brine and, tomorrow, bring a truck with five thousand kilograms of sardines. I want to try out the pressure cookers. Notify the women who were working here."

Señor López told me, "Monsieur Duchateau wants you to stay here until everything is ready. I am going to take you to the café 'Le Glacier' so you can spend a little time with your compatriots. Later, you will come back here by taxi because I am on duty starting at midday."

There at "Le Glacier," all my acquaintances were waiting for me impatiently, even Señor González Sicilia, who had been the governor of Seville. Our chat lasted until almost two in the afternoon.[21] My compatriots were amazed that I, who had barely set foot in Casablanca, was already involved in a job about which I knew nothing. They said I had a lot of guts, because, even though I may have been born in a cannery, I had never worked as a canner. I replied that I had no other recourse but to take a chance at running a factory. It was either that or abject poverty, and I was not prepared to live as a beggar if I thought I could earn a living by my own efforts. In the same café, I ordered

---
21 He is referring to Ramón González Sicilia de la Corte. This lawyer, professor, and Freemason served as a deputy to parliament representing Seville, first as a member of the Radical Party and later as a member of the Republican Union Party. On April 14, 1931, with the proclamation of the Second Spanish Republic, he was designated provisional civil governor of the province of Seville. From there, he assumed the presidency of the Seville Provincial Government and later became the civil governor of Granada. Also during the Republic, he was the consul in Casablanca. Eventually, he served in the same city as the representative of JARE (Junta for the Aid of Spanish Refugees), a post which would later enable him to obtain from the French authorities the legalization of many undocumented refugees, among them the anarchist leader Cipriano Mera Sanz.

a sandwich of ham and eggs, and, once I had devoured it, I had them call for a taxi. Then I returned to the factory.

Poor Da Rosa

At the factory, I began running around giving orders as if I had been doing it all my life. A Portuguese lady, who looked to be in her fifties, came to see me and was astonished when I answered her in correct Portuguese. She was the wife of Armando Da Rosa, the factory's technician, who was in the hospital suffering from cancer. This woman came to ask me not to take her husband's job if he returned, because they were very poor and had five small children. I told her, "Look, Señora, I promise you that the moment your husband comes through that door, I will be on my way. Trust me, because I never go back on my word."

I was talking to her when Monsieur Duchateau appeared. She left at once. He asked me, "What was that about?"

"Nothing important," I answered. "It was the technician's wife, who has pleaded with me not to take her husband's job."

"Don't believe a thing. Her husband is at death's door. We are taking steps with the Portuguese Consulate to have him hospitalized in his own country. Don't worry. He's not coming back."

When I had been at the factory almost a month, I had become more and more involved in the company's management. Everything was going *"merveilleusement,"* as Monsieur Duchateau said. We had doubled production.

One afternoon at about four o'clock, I was about to celebrate this success when I saw a pale, nearly skeletal man enter through the factory's large door. He came straight to me and, without introducing himself, said in a voice that trembled, either with anger or fear, I don't know which, "Get out of here. This is my factory and my livelihood and my children's sustenance. You have come to steal my happiness."

What could I say to poor Da Rosa? Monsieur Duchateau had told me that this man was an illiterate and that, with him, they had never been able to turn out more than five thousand kilos a day, while with me, production had doubled and labor costs had fallen.

"Please, Da Rosa, calm down," I told him in Portuguese. "Stay here. I am leaving at once. When the owner comes, tell him not to look for me. You have come back and I quit. Good-by."

I went out the factory door and walked back to the hotel, where I changed out of my work clothes. After washing up, I went to the café "Le Glacier," where, as usual, my compatriots were playing dominoes. I took Don Pablo aside and explained my ethical dilemma to him. He called me a fool and said we were living through a time of war and I should not have such asinine scruples. I refused to say where I was going. As darkness fell, I gathered my suitcase, paid my hotel bill, and, a hundred kilometers later, I was in Rabat.

With my inseparable suitcase in hand, I went into a café-restaurant called "Des Malles." Behind the counter was the owner, an aging legionnaire of Spanish origin. I ordered a coffee with milk and told him I was a refugee. I asked him to tell me where I could find a cheap hotel for the night. He asked me about my political ideas and I told him, "I am a Socialist."

He went to the other end of the counter and spoke to an elegantly dressed French gentleman, who then approached me. He interrogated me extensively and asked me for my papers. I thought he was a member of the secret police. We sat down together at a table and he said, "I am going to solve your problem right away. In a few minutes, a Spanish refugee who lives in our Socialist club, the 'Roger Salengro Circle,' is coming here to eat."

"How happy you have made me," I replied.

"It is a duty we French Socialists have toward pro-democratic Spaniards, whom we regard as our brothers," this friend said. "My name is Jean Leonetti, and I am a deputy. Look, here comes your comrade whom we protect, Antonio Calzado García."

After we were introduced, Calzado was informed, to his surprise, that I was going to live with him in the "Roger Salengro Circle," and would be coming to eat at this restaurant belonging to Antonio Espinosa, 'The Legionnaire' as he was called, all at the expense of our French comrades. Antonio Calzado told me about his service during the war on a hospital train and described the time he later spent in France in the camp for Spanish refugees at Argelès sur Mer. After eating, we walked to the Circle, about eight hundred meters from the restaurant. We were up late into the night telling each other our troubles. Almost all the comrades were employees or functionaries of the French government in Morocco. Needless to say, there was a world of difference between Spanish socialism and the French variety. Here they all had an automobile, a chalet, and a style of life completely different from that of the hungry Spanish workers, poorly shod in their hemp-soled canvas shoes, who filled our ranks. Upon hearing of my arrival, the members of the Circle showed up to meet me and offer me their houses. How pleased they were that I could converse with them in their language. I had recently been speaking a lot of French with Monsieur Duchateau, who often corrected my pronunciation, and this had served me well.

I was incapable of remaining idle, and so I spent my time writing. I composed a novel I called *Malapata* [Bad Luck]. While Calzado and his friends played cards or dominoes, I would sit in the corner of some café and write whatever my imagination dictated. The Spanish Republican Home for Displaced Children was here in Rabat and I wrote a comic one-act play for them in the Andalusian style. I entitled it "Juan Carrizo's Patio."

Señor López showed up and he was furious with me for abandoning the canning factory, which Monsieur Duchateau had been forced to close for good. I set forth all the arguments I could, based on humanitarian considerations and pity for the unfortunate Da Rosa, but to no avail. All López knew was the sacred duty of profit.

The European War

During our civil war, France and England had been very fearful that if they helped the Spanish "reds," it could cause a war with Germany, which had armed itself to the teeth, something the democratic nations had not done. The latter put more trust in their treaties with the Germans than in the manufacture of war materiel, an attitude they maintained right up to September 1939, when the news arrived that Hitler had declared war. I saw my French friends crying when they heard the news.

After that, trains could be seen leaving Rabat filled with people called up by the French government to swell the ranks of the French army and defend the nation. The French Socialists met and proceeded to close the "Roger Salengro Circle."

They notified us that they were abandoning the locale and distributing the furniture among those who had spacious chalets. One of our comrades told us, "This is war. We have to think only of the homeland and its defense. If you wish, you can come with me. I will sign you up in the Foreign Legion."

My friend Calzado, who was sharper than I was about such matters, replied, "We will have to think about it." Later Calzado told me, "They say we have only three choices: the Legion, the cemetery in our hometowns, or a concentration camp. I don't intend to take any of those routes. Starting tonight, I am sleeping at the house of one of my friends."

"Well," I told him as I packed my suitcase, "I am leaving right now for Casablanca. I will try to remake my life in that big city. I have confidence in myself. Since you are staying here, pass on my gratitude to those who have helped us. I will write you from there and let you know how things are going in 'refugeeland.'"

I went to the café "Le Glacier," where my compatriots were preparing to flee to Mexico, despite the danger posed by German submarines. One of the regulars at the café, who knew of my initiatives in the canning industry, proposed we visit the "Rambou and Menaud" transport company. They had built a new garage for their trucks and had abandoned the locale they had in Roches Lloires, which would be a magnificent place for a small factory for salt-curing sardines. The following morning, I was at the company office. I don't know whether the director thought I was joking or serious, but he had me sign a rental contract for two hundred and fifty francs a month and handed me the keys to the old garage. I went to the house of a refugee named José Vivas, who had a large family. I explained my plan to manufacture salt-cured sardines, which were consumed in great quantities in Casablanca and the surrounding area.

The same day, we went and opened the garage. It was a magnificent place for my project. It even had electricity and running water. Señor Pastor, a retired railroad employee, lent us two thousand francs. A baker lent us another thousand, and within a week, the first two brine vats were built. We bought several sacks of salt, and a few days later, the first sardines we bought in the Port of Casablanca came through the door. In the first month, there were already fourteen undocumented refugees working in our cooperative. I bought some worm gears and used them to construct a press. The oldest of us, whom I still remember for his generosity, was named Cipriano Mera Sanz. During the war, he had become famous for leading an anarchist militia when the Italians were defeated at the battle of Guadalajara. Cipriano had no documents because he had escaped from a jail in Algeria, where he had been under arrest. He was well hidden with us. By that time we were even making anchovy rolls fried in oil.

One fine day, or I should say one bad day, an official from the Casablanca city hall showed up and gave us an order from the municipality demanding we close the factory because, according to the new zoning law, our factory was located two hundred meters outside the industrial zone. The official advised us to finish and sell the products we had. He gave us fifteen days to comply. Our appeals and entreaties were in vain. We all looked for premises in that industrial zone where we could continue our business. Our efforts were futile. We settled our debt with Señor Pastor, interest free, and I decided to look for a job, which I found right away.

Once again, I was working in a canning factory, but this time it was necessary to put in longer hours. Everything we could produce was already sold to France. If the war lasted a long time, the whole country was going to go hungry. Fish trucks would be coming from Casablanca, from Safi, or from any fishing port that could provide a daily supply. "I am putting you in charge of the whole factory," Monsieur Mallein told me. "I will handle only exporting and finances."

The drivers, mechanics, stokers, and all the specialists were Spanish refugees, among them two brothers from the Canary Islands. I put in eighteen- or twenty-hour days. I didn't sit down even for a ten-minute rest. It was the energy of youth.

With General Pétain's armistice and the German occupation of France, the so-called German Commission arrived in Casablanca to take command of Morocco. The noose around the Spanish refugees began to close, because the Germans thought we could perhaps help the allied forces in the event of a landing in North Africa. And since Franco was a friend of Hitler, the Germans would have to cooperate with the Spanish government's wishes. Those like me who were dedicating all of our time to work did not grasp the situation. Spain was so dangerously close. Consequently, the more prominent Spanish Republicans, aided by the international powers, were being evacuated to South America.

One of those days, I received an order to report to the Central Police Headquarters at four o'clock in the afternoon. I asked Monsieur Mallein to find me a substitute until I returned. There were three hundred women and twenty-four men milling about. I made my way to the office indicated on the order. After taking my identification, a police officer jolted me with the horrific phrase, "You are under arrest."

"Me?" I replied. "But why?"

"Ah, my friend," the policeman told me, "don't blame us. They are orders from the German Commission and we must respect them, whether we like it or not."

"And where are they taking us?"

"It could be anywhere. One thing is certain. It will be far from Casablanca."

"Alright," I said bitterly, "I beg you to please call Monsieur Mallein at the factory and tell him I have been arrested, because the factory is in operation right now and under my responsibility."

He went out into the corridor and returned with a uniformed policeman and handed me over to his custody. At that moment, I understood that my drama had just begun. I followed the policeman, who took me down a long corridor to the headquarters' interior courtyard, where there were already some fifty refugees who were going to suffer the same fate as me. As night fell, they called for me. I had a glimmer of hope as I was taken to a different office. Monsieur Mallein was there and he was furious about my arrest. I begged him to send me my suitcase because I needed a change of clothing. He promised me he would get me out as soon as possible. I was taken away, but not back to the patio. They put me in a cell full of other Spanish refugees. We introduced ourselves to each other and became acquainted with those we hadn't met until then. The cell door opened and a policeman handed me my suitcase and, along with it, an envelope containing fifty thousand francs, a small fortune at the time.

We spent the night locked up there. Whenever someone said we were going to be returned to Spain, my hair would stand on end. Many had enlisted in the Foreign Legion to avoid that eventuality. Better to die in a skirmish than to be taken in cold blood and shot by the wall of some town's cemetery. Most of the refugees in the cell said, "If I had known this, they wouldn't have caught me." They brought each of us a small roll with cooked ham and some bottles of mineral water. As the saying goes, in hard times put on a good face. There were some in the cell who began telling jokes to cheer up their unfortunate compatriots. The night before, I had only slept four hours, but now I wasn't even sleepy. It was a repetition of the same syndrome as when I was being pursued in Spain. By the end of the night, there were some who were snoring as they lay on those reed mats which were the only furniture in the cells.

Before dawn we heard voices and footsteps approaching from down the corridor. Soon the gendarmes arrived and unlocked the cell doors. A policeman read from a list, "So and so, son of José and Ana." The one whose name was read had to respond with, "Present." I trembled with fear, recalling what I had been told of the famous lists read aloud in the jails of Spanish towns as a prelude to another mass assassination. As we left the cell, we were handcuffed, two by two.

"This doesn't look good," said one of the prisoners.

"Do you think these guys are really going to take us to Spain?" said another.

"If they take us to Tangiers, we will have to put up a fight," said a loud voice that the gendarmes, in an authoritarian tone, ordered to shut up.

"Silence," they said.

I shared my handcuffs with a man in his fifties named Antonio Fernández, from Seville, who had set up an olive factory in Casablanca. He had been arrested as he worked. There were shoemakers from Elche, who had just begun to be successful and had sent for their wives and children, and others who began by melting scrap aluminum and had everything ready to forge spoons and forks, in great demand here. These French gendarmes who were collaborating with the German Commission were going to disrupt these poor men's plans to earn a living.

"How shameless!" said my companion Fernández. "When I get out of this one, I'm going back to Spain. Never in my life have I been jailed before and handcuffed, just like a thief. First these Frenchmen save our lives and then they feed us to the wolves."

An abrupt order could be heard, "Prisoners, calm down." Every minute our ears were wounded by that word, "prisoners." The time to leave arrived. Where would they take us? My right hand was chained to Señor Fernández, and with my left I held onto my suitcase. We were marched two kilometers to the train station, where there were almost a hundred people who had come to say good-by to their loved ones. Some of the prisoners had already brought their wives and children to Casablanca. Others had fiancées here and were planning their weddings. I wondered who had notified these relatives. Coldly and without scruples, the gendarmes prevented all conversation and contact. They even insulted us. Finally, the train arrived. They ordered us aboard. If someone had to use the toilet, he couldn't do so without towing his companion along while a gendarme kept watch.

The train stopped at a station whose sign read Oued-Zem. We got off and formed a column that marched to a camp composed of a quadrilateral of barracks. We entered the central courtyard where the French flag was flying. There, we were ordered to line up in formation. They read the list again and we had to respond with the ritual "Present." After the list was read, our handcuffs were removed and we breathed a sigh of relief.

The camp's captain and his subordinates came to greet us. I remember well what he said: "Sirs, I greet you as gentlemen and not as men who have been vanquished. On my part, you will have all the facilities you require, within the limitations of the present circumstances. This is a camp for the selection or triage of those persons fit for manual labor. Therefore, I ask that you maintain order and discipline as if this were a military training camp until the commission makes a determination in each of your cases. I ask you not to attempt to escape. If that happens, I will be obliged to take other measures which, for the moment, I would prefer to avoid."

After that proper greeting, which filled us with hope, we were taken to the barracks. In each room, there were fifteen bunks on each side and a corridor down the middle. The bunks were numbered. I chose one near the center of the room and put my little suitcase under it. This had been a camp for the Foreign Legion, which had been taken to France to prevent the Germans from entering that country. An army officer came in and ordered us to sit down on our respective bunks. Then he made a list of all those who belonged to this module. When he finished, we went to the mess hall, where they served us a succulent plate of potatoes with meat and chorizo, a glass of good wine, and a roll.

That night, with the lights turned off, we told each other innumerable jokes that provoked hearty laughter. That same night, two young Communists escaped. During the next morning roll call, when their names were read out, their friends responded with a "Present." Days later, when the soldiers discovered what had happened, they ordered us to sit on our bunks. That way they could ascertain how many were missing and who they were. From then on, the camp was surrounded by barbed wire, which was also installed in the barrack windows and around the doors. They assigned several Moroccan guards to watch us night and day. What could have been pleasant days were turned into a living hell. Nevertheless, I maintained my good spirits. I was always together with Ramón Peña, the former diplomat, who had requested asylum in Mexico. Once again we spent the nights telling jokes to make the more desperate of us laugh.

There was an epidemic of dysentery and, since there were only two toilets, many men dirtied their pants as they waited in the interminable lines.

When we had been there fifteen days, the German commission arrived and we were given medical examinations to determine who was fit and who was unfit for manual labor. The following day, a list was posted with the names of those who had been rented out by the "Industrial Production and Labor" service to a French firm, the Mediterranean-Niger Company, which was to build the Trans-Saharan railroad. Since my name was on the list, I presented my safe-conduct pass expedited in Portugal, which said, "In transit through Casablanca en route to Mexico." I also showed them the money Monsieur Mallein had given me. They filled out some forms for my departure and an application to the Mexican Embassy in Paris. But meanwhile...

At dawn on the following day, I found myself once again with my suitcase in my left hand and, on my right, handcuffs that bound me to Mascarel. He was one of the men who would one day plant the orange groves that brought so many benefits to Morocco. As I had already foreseen, a column of "prisoners" was formed and boarded on a train bound for Fez, where we arrived that afternoon. They ordered us off the train and marched us to the jail of that Moroccan capital.

I was beginning to enjoy this adventure and the discovery of new lands and new horizons. I was no longer responsible for factories, boilers, pressure cookers, and so many other dangerous steam-driven machines. Nor did I have to deal with personnel problems. All I had to do was take care of myself.

We entered the Fez jail. Those who had wives and children were in a state of high anxiety. All one could hear were lamentations and, "Tomorrow, I am going to write to the consul." I realized that our cell was infected with bedbugs. I made a circle of water and sat down in the middle of the cell on my suitcase. I spent the night with my cheek resting on my hand until morning, when they brought us watered-down coffee. Then there was the familiar routine of being handcuffed and marched in a column of prisoners back to the train station and boarded on a car under the hostile gaze of the French gendarmes. After that, we traveled for hours and hours across a semi-desert plain.

At last we arrived in Oujda. This is the gateway to the desert on the Algerian border. Then, always in handcuffs, they took us from the train to the jail, where we spent the night. This was the third prison we visited. The bitterness of my fellow prisoners was visible in their faces, especially those who had family responsibilities and whose worries must have been horrible. And those responsible for this tragedy were governing Spain with the aid of Italy,

Germany, Portugal, and the Moors, and with the blessings of the Pope.

That night I slept well until they took us out in the morning and ordered us to extend our arms so they could handcuff us again. Why repeat this order? We were already accustomed to the routine. Formed into a double column, we were marched to the station and a train that would take us from Oujda to Bouarfa, some five hundred kilometers into the desert. That is what we were told by an employee of the Algerian railroad whose name was Baños. He was from Cartagena. He told us the climate was pleasant in Bouarfa and that we would find ourselves among some two thousand Spaniards who had come through Algeria and were building the Trans-Saharan railroad.

Duly handcuffed and guarded by other gendarmes, we took our places in the cars reserved for "prisoners." Before our arrival, they were already partly occupied by prisoners from other countries who had fled the war. Morocco, Algeria, and even Tunisia were getting rid of foreigners by sending us to the Mediterranean-Niger Company, where we would be used to construct that railroad across the desert. We crossed an immense plain of red earth, dabbed here and there with thickets of coarse grass. Occasionally, groups of nomads could be seen with their herds of goats and camels. We made a stop in front of the Jerada coal mines, a magnificent industrial complex in the middle of the desert. After that, we passed through the Ganfuda region, where there were herds of gazelles that, startled by the presence of the train, leaped about like enormous fleas.

Among the passengers there were two, who, in plain view of everyone, were playing cards for enormous sums of money. Jean Davica and Rabinovieh, as they introduced themselves to us, were Yugoslavians of Jewish origin. They preferred adventure to war and were in the same situation as our own. I was reading a novel by Henri Mordeaux, *La Maison*, when one of the gendarmes approached and asked me, "Do you read French?"

"*Oui, monsieur*," I replied, "*et je parle aussi presque bien*."

My conversation with this gendarme was fairly extensive. I informed him that those he had been ordered to transport to Bouarfa were not soldiers. On the contrary, we were almost all civilians and there were many among us who were heads of families. It was because we refused to live in a military dictatorship that we were in this sad situation. When he found out I was the manager of the factory that produced "Unica" sardines, he was astonished and asked, "*Mais pourquoi vous se trouvez ici?*" I explained what the Casablanca police had said about the famous German Commission.

In Bouarfa, Desert Capital

Night was falling when the train stopped in the Bouarfa station. It was in a mountain of buttresses in the Anti Atlas range. That was where the workshops, bakeries, warehouses, and garages were, and all the necessities for a project of such magnitude as the construction of hundreds of kilometers of rail lines in the middle of a desert. We got off the train and marched in a double column, handcuffed two by two just as we had been since Oujda, until we came to an immense cave under an enormous cliff. We passed through a double line of Arab soldiers armed with rifles, who guarded the edges of the road to the mouth of the cave, where gendarmes removed our handcuffs. The cave entrance consisted of a metal grill so that air could pass through.

We were all apprehensive. Suddenly, from the back of the cave, there was a roar of laughter. We were perplexed. There was a crude wooden table with an oil lamp that illuminated the large space, allowing us to see the fear in our companions' faces. The roar of laughter rang out again, even louder. A man emerged wearing the tattered remnants of an old French Foreign Legion uniform and sporting a long disheveled beard. He was laughing as if he were mad. "So, you have arrived. Here are the rich kids who were strolling about Casablanca. Now you will find out what work is. They've locked me up here for refusing to work."

And he started laughing again.

We didn't respond. We were terrified. Suddenly, a fly flew into the oil lamp and snuffed it out. Someone struck a match and relit it. There was that dirty ragged man facing us. "I am called 'Shrapnel,'" he said and laughed again.

We all looked at one another. Mascarel never left my side. He told me he had the impression we had fallen into the cruelest madhouse ever built by mankind. More flies were coming in through the metal grating and extinguishing the lamp.

Meanwhile, 'Shrapnel' kept laughing and making my companions increasingly nervous. We were brought a little roll for each of us, a pail of boiled unpeeled potatoes and a boiled egg. Those who worked in the Bouarfa kitchen tent were all Spaniards. They answered anything we asked them and told us that in the morning they would let us out and take us in groups to the places where we had to work.

I was examining the oil lamp, which was nothing more than a glass jar that had once been an inkwell and to whose lid a small tube about two centimeters long had been soldered. A wick passed through this tube, soaking up diesel fuel provided by the truck drivers for the Trans-Saharan railroad, who were all Spanish. This was the only illumination for that tragic and fantastic scene.

On the other side of the cave door, there was an Arab soldier, rifle at the ready, and it was through that door or grate that the swift desert flies entered and headed straight into the lamp's flame, extinguishing it. Another match and the light went on again so we could get a good look at all the sad faces.

'Shrapnel's' laughter and jests did not last long. He soon realized that he had nothing to gain by making fun of other people's misery, because it was his misery as well. Then he tried to explain to us how things worked in these concentration camps, which went by the deceitful name of the "Industrial Production and Labor" service that, for a few measly francs, had battalions of men who were paid only in food that was barely enough to survive the arduous labor.

'Shrapnel' told us, "These camps are run like genuine military dictatorships, even though there are neither soldiers nor arms. If you escape, there is only the desert, and it is unlikely you will ever get across it. At night, the jackals, and there are thousands of them, will surround you and wait for one of them to attack so the rest can do the same. They give you a cubic meter of stones to break up for the railroad bed. All you have is a little hammer that we call a truncheon and, at dawn, after a legionnaire plays reveille, they give you a light breakfast of coffee with milk, line you up in the camp's yard where the French colors are flying, and from there it's off to the quarry. You are under constant surveillance. If you commit some transgression or some act they consider defiant of their authority, or if you disobey their orders, they arrest you and send you here, and from here they send you to the disciplinary zone on the edge of the desert. Some have to dig a grave and lie down in it, and if you try to raise your head or draw up your legs, there is an Arab nearby with a basket of stones to throw at the poor man condemned to such a cruel punishment. One had to have his toes amputated because they had become frozen in the bitter winter night of the desert. Another punishment is to tie your hands to the tail of a horse and make it run around the camp. If the person falls, he is dragged behind the animal. The camp directors and guards are foreign officers from the disbanded Legion. They are naturalized French citizens and have military habits and souls. Tomorrow, they will call you one by one and give you sandals and clothing, and then they will take you to your assigned companies. Whoever enters there, will never get out alive."

What an unpleasant night! In a cave with a ragged and half-crazed Spanish refugee, with a lamp that the flies extinguished every ten minutes, and waiting for our dreadful integration into a company of *travailleurs étrangers* to break rocks. I am wondering where it will all lead. As usual, I sit on my suitcase with my back against the wall and, with my elbow on my knee, I rest my face on my right hand. I slept that way until a sharp pain in my wrist woke me up. It was almost daybreak. Some were sleeping huddled on coarse straw mats. Light filtered in through the metal grill so I could see the human shapes of those men who had not robbed or killed anyone. Almost eighty percent of them had never even handled a gun. Here we were in the middle of the twentieth century, workers rented out against our will with the blessings of Italian Fascists, Hitler's National Socialists, and international consortiums. What a way for the world to be arranged!

Into the Desert

In the morning, we were called one at a time and taken to the company's central office. "Name, trade, religion, political affiliation."

We all said, "Republican, Catholic."

Then we were taken to a warehouse where they gave us sandals fashioned from truck tires by "prisoners," used clothing handed down by the Legion, a tin plate, a spoon, and a fork. It was the last time we were all together. They divided us into groups and sent us to the different companies or work battalions. There were ten of us loaded on a truck with other foreigners. Each group had its own equipment.

The first stop was in Mengoub, a camp set up near a well dug by refugees from Valencia, from which surged a miraculous abundance of excellent drinking water, the contents of a subterranean river that flowed from the Atlas Mountains and had been swallowed up by a desert with centuries of thirst. They dropped off a mail sack and a few of the workers. Then we headed deeper into the desert along a reddish and dusty road that ran parallel to the rail line that was being constructed. They had given us a small sack of provisions that I nibbled on with little appetite. I was seated in the truck bed next to my suitcase that served me as an armrest. I remained in that position without speaking to anyone, because they were all strangers to me, until we arrived at kilometer eighty-six, about six hundred kilometers from Oujda, according to my calculations. The truck stopped, and a Spaniard, who must have been the truck's mechanic, told me to take my things and get off. I did as he ordered. As I unloaded my baggage, I saw with surprise that someone had stolen my stylish sandals.

Two or three men approached. I was the only passenger destined for this camp. One of the men came up to me and the others took an envelope from the driver. It probably contained the documents concerning my assignment. The man who received me spoke in correct Spanish. He told me to follow him and led me to a large tent. He asked me if I was a Socialist and I told him I was.

"This is your home. It has four cots. Three are occupied and the fourth is yours. The sack that is on your cot will be your mattress. You need to fill it with the dry grass that grows around here. Tomorrow you will not work. You will spend the day getting established and being properly identified. We have your medical record and other documents pertaining to you. I am going to give you a small sickle so you can cut grass and fill your sack before sundown. The boys are at the quarry and will be returning soon."

"Can I leave my suitcase here?" I inquired.

"Yes. Don't worry about it. There is no one in the camp now." This company was the Second. That's what it was called. Second Company, consisting of a small yard in whose center the French flag was waving. The rectangle that formed the yard was defined by large tents pitched over areas dug one meter deep. In each tent there were four cots: a rectangle of poles and four legs. The rectangles supported a metal screen of chicken wire. That is where I had to put my "mattress," or sack full of dry grass, which I cut with the haste of someone in unknown territory, fearful of encountering some wild animal. In less than half an hour I was heading back to my "domicile" with my mattress on my head, when I saw the group of "rented workers" returning from the quarry. The railroad station was next to the tent, which left a poor impression, but I did not have much time to think about it because the "battalion" was almost back, moving slowly, the men tired from their day's work, dressed in the castoff garments of the Legion: brown or dark green coats.

Three men entered the tent. I arrived with my sack of dry grass, sharp as needles, and placed this mattress on my assigned bed. We immediately struck up a conversation. The first of my tent mates was Antonio Iglesias, who had been the mayor of Almonte, in the province of Huelva, and later commissar in the Republican army; the second was Pedro Rodríguez, from Puebla de Guzmán; and the third, another Andalusian, was known as 'The Border Guard.'

We had a lot to talk about. They wanted to hear what I had to say because they had come from "the other side," meaning they had been in the Republican zone, and needed to know what had happened in the zone controlled by Franco's forces, and I wanted to hear what they had to say for the same reason. Antonio Iglesias told me that among the refugees in the camp there were certain individuals who were dangerous thieves and innate shirkers. "The true worker labors for the pleasure it gives him to be useful and productive, to give free rein and satisfaction to his muscles and body. He devotes himself to the effort without thinking about whether he is paid well or poorly. The shirker is of no use to any political party or regime. He is never content or of service to humanity. The true worker eats in moderation. He is happy with whatever winds up in his stomach and doesn't complain about it. The shirker is a glutton who is never satisfied."

I have calculated where we are. Some two hundred meters from the camp, there was a straight and level line raised a meter and a half above the plain. It was the bed along which the Mediterranean-Niger Railroad would run for about one hundred and eighty kilometers, until it reached the Kenadsa coal fields that had been discovered on the edge of the desert. Young Spaniards who say they had driven tanks or trucks were the ones who operated the tractors, graders, excavators, and other mechanical devices. In an incessant coming and going, they were constructing kilometers and kilometers of railroad bed and then laying the tracks.

We spent part of the night telling each other our stories. They had already spent considerable time in these battalions of *travailleurs étrangers*. It was from them I found out that Manuel Flores Rodríguez, the mayor of Ayamonte, and Miguel Gómez Barranco, also from my hometown, were working a few kilometers further down the line. They were with another battalion that was working from south to north in this direction to join up with us. This would take several months.

It occurred to me to say, "By that time I won't be here." My three companions burst out laughing, which left me perplexed.

"What a dreamer," Iglesias told me. "Whoever enters here never gets out. Do you think you have landed in friendly territory? Get used to the idea that you have been sold the way gypsies sell a burro."

"Antonio," I said, "I don't think I'll be here with you more than two or three months. Just enough time to write my impressions of this life you're leading. I am hoping to leave for Mexico or continue my work in the production of food, so badly needed in France."

"If only it were so," said Pedro Rodríguez. "If you get out, do what you can to take some of us with you. We are resigned by now and without hope."

Time to rest. Everyone sleeps. I am trying to get my body used to this mattress of dry grass. One blade has stuck me in the arm, and I pull on it until I remove it from the sack. A pack of jackals prowls among the tents looking for something to quiet their hunger. The cold is unbearable. I can't sleep while these accursed jackals keep up their pitiful howls. I notice that everyone else is fast asleep. The jackals pass a half meter from my head. I think they are even sniffing at the canvas of our tent. I have a box of matches in my left hand and a candle stub in the other, just in case.

I've nodded off a few times and at dawn the bugle blows reveille. Everyone wakes up and goes out to wash. There are two large iron cisterns about three meters high that are kept full by tanker trucks.

"You need to bring your towel, comb, soap, and toothbrush," Antonio Iglesias tells me.

After washing up, it's back "home." This morning it is the turn of 'The Border Guard' to bring coffee with milk and a small roll.

Rassemblement

A booming voice has given the order for formation. From the tents, workers are emerging and lining up in front of the pole on which the French flag will soon be waving. There are about a hundred men with tangled hair and dressed in overcoats cast off by the Foreign Legion. Some of the men have removed the sleeve linings and put them on their feet like socks to withstand the insufferable cold. Each man has a carafe or bottle full of water. These containers wrapped in damp rags will be buried, hidden in a shady spot, to protect them from the sun which, by ten in the morning, will be scorching.

The salute to the flag. A worker slowly raises the French flag. Everyone has to remove their hat. The camp captain and officers come to attention and give a military salute. The column begins its trek to the workplace. It was upsetting to see that column of men dressed in rags. I had only seen such a sight at the cinema in a moving picture: *Napoleon's Defeat at Waterloo*. The interpreter told me, "You stay here today. You have to go to the office for identification and classification." And so it was. The staff has joined Captain Brunikel for my interrogation.

The captain, of Polish origin, is astonished that I address him in correct French.

"Miguel," he said, "are you a worker or an intellectual?"

"I am an intellectual worker," I replied.

"Does such a thing exist?" he said in amazement.

"It is possible," I responded. *"L'ouvrier peut étudier après son adolescence et reussier a avoir une situation convenable en la société* [The worker can study after adolescence and aspire to have an appropriate place in society]."

The conversation continued until, at last, the interpreter told me, "You will have to break up a cubic meter of stones for the railroad bed every day."

"I will do what I can," I told him.

I left and went to my "house." I opened my suitcase. Under my bed, I dug a hole. After wrapping my capital in a handkerchief, I buried it. It was the capital Monsieur Mallein had given me: fifty thousand francs. It was what I imagined a ticket to Mexico would cost.

Meanwhile, I was rejoined by those *travailleurs étrangers* who, like me, slept on bristly mattresses without sheets or blankets. At my side was Antonio Iglesias, the man who had wanted to have the picture of the Virgin removed from the meeting room of his town hall and was nearly thrown from the balcony.[22]

---

[22] This is a reference to a serious incident organized by anti-Republican sectors from Seville and Huelva in response to the removal of the paintings of the Sacred Heart and of the Virgin of Rocío from the meeting room of the Almonte Town Hall, images that were placed there during the last days of the dictatorship of Miguel Primo de Rivera. The Antonio Iglesias referred to by Domínguez Soler must be Antonio Iglesias Báñez, councilman during the first Republican biennium and during the months of the Popular Front government. The mayor of Almonte at the time was Fernando Villarán Morales.

Work

Breaking rocks. They had to be broken down to five centimeters in order to create a bed on which to lay the rails. There was a foreman who, according to what they said, had been a sergeant in the Spanish army. His name, or maybe his surname, was Ximeno. 'The Border Guard' grabbed a "truncheon"—a small-headed hammer with a long handle—placed his foot on a rock and, with a few blows, made it explode into three or four pieces. Pedro Rodríguez and I, with our little "truncheons," had to break up the cubic meter of rocks we had each been allotted. First rock. I took it into my hands. It seemed like child's play. I struck it, smack, smack, smack, and the rock did not explode. I felt like I was hitting a rugby ball.

By ten o'clock, the sun was beating down on the place where we were working. The whole panorama had changed completely. The men began to strip down completely. Off came the coats, off came the shirts. Naked from the waist up and back to work. I stripped down as well. Suddenly, the heat was unbearable. Thousands of desert flies were biting the corners of our eyes and the edges of our lips. It was an insufferable torment. We were batting at our faces. And those flies, about half the size of the common flies we are used to, would rather be crushed to death by our knuckles than let go of the flesh they were biting. It was as though our very being was being inundated by a nervous attack we had never experienced before. I continue striking the rocks. 'The Border Guard,' without speaking to anyone, kept on holding down rocks with his left foot and, with one blow of his truncheon, would break each rock into three pieces.

By midday my throat felt as if it were a dry reed. I needed to become adapted to this work. Every once in a while I would glance at the pile of rocks I was supposed to break and it would spur me to work with greater determination in order to complete the task I had been assigned. Some of the men would give me advice. "Strike it here." "Strike it there." At noon we went back to the camp to eat. Each day it was someone else's turn to serve the food and wash the plates and spoons.

In my suitcase, I have my tall rubber boots that I wore when I worked in the factory. They had been ordered for me by 'Little Stump.' He was a refugee named Francisco Molina Aguilar, born in Campo de Gibraltar. His mother had a second husband who was British. That is how these English boots arrived in Casablanca by mail. 'Little Stump' and I went to the post office to pick them up. My friend was a disabled soldier but, although he belonged to that category, he never received a penny in compensation. "Curro Molina," as the Andalusian song goes, "even he would have shed tears if he knew my dreadful fate." A grenade had gone off in his hand, and he was always thinking of that bitter hour when he had argued with his wife and slapped her face. She had cursed him saying, "May God break the hand with which you have hit me." While I was working, he lacked nothing. Now he is probably one more derelict in that heterogeneous world where each man fends for himself.

They say that many of those in the camp steal whatever they can and sell it to the Moroccans. Consequently, when I came out wearing these magnificent boots, I was called to the office to see whether the boots were from the Mediterranean-Niger warehouses. When the captain saw they were of English origin, he asked me if I had relations or correspondence with the English. I had to explain my friendship with Francisco Molina and how, through this friendship, I was able to acquire the boots.

Our comrade, Mas, was the mailman of the company, and I began handing my letters over to him. Each day I would write to someone. Upon returning from work that first afternoon, and after the lowering of the flag and the daily report with orders from the "Industrial Production and Labor" service, we returned to our tents. 'The Border Guard' grabbed a mattock and I brought a sack. Night was coming on. What were we looking for? 'The Border Guard' went to a place where there were minuscule desert flowers. He stuck his mattock a few times into the reddish ground around the plant and extracted a nearly petrified black root some twenty-five centimeters long and seven centimeters thick. "Put it in the sack," he told me. He stuck his mattock in again and got another root that I threw into the sack. We kept at it until we had gathered all we needed.

When we got back to the tent, Pedro Rodríguez laid out a piece of a metal barrel, arranged the roots on it, and lit them. Within half an hour, those roots had become embers that would keep us warm all night. I was amazed at how one could find everything one needed in nature if you knew how to look. The desert was intensely cold by that late October, but the fuel we needed was barely fifty meters from our tent. With a piece of metal screen that was once part of an oil filter from a truck, I fashioned a protective cover for my oil lamp so the flies wouldn't extinguish it and I could write. In this way, I was writing two letters a day.

When my work was measured at the end of the week, I had averaged eighty centimeters, almost the meter demanded of me. The foreman congratulated me. It was a record for a beginner at that work. And that was in spite of the time I was losing rubbing my eyes and mouth with my knuckles to kill the flies. There were always fresh reinforcements to replace the dead. Some of them would even crawl up my nostrils. Their bites would drive me insane.

There we were with one foot in the Sahara desert, from whose interior powerful windstorms would come. They raised immense curtains of red sand that would fill the horizon all the way up the sky. It was an imposing sight to see those clouds advancing toward us until they swallowed everything. We would take down the center pole of our tents and disappear into the holes that had been dug a meter deep underneath those shelters as a precautionary measure against these storms with their asphyxiating smell. Nevertheless, on those nights, just as on the other nights when the moon was so clear you could see the desert ants walking about, the jackals, sometimes accompanied by hyenas, continued howling their hungry serenades.

Sunday was our day off, our day of rest. In the morning, I spent the time filling up pages, writing either letters or articles about my impressions of this place. In the afternoon, I would sometimes go to the camp of the legionnaires that was a few kilometers distance from ours. They had set up a cantina that had fine food they brought in from Algeria, as well as cigarettes of excellent quality. Other times, I would hike some two and a half kilometers away from our camp. There, in the middle of the plain, was a hill that rose almost a hundred and fifty meters and had a sort of valley in its center. This hill consisted of enormous crags, as if it had fallen there from some star. I would climb to the summit, from which I contemplated the horizon, a magnificent panorama without undulations, full of crows and mystery. It was like the horizon at sea, but without clouds, seagulls, or ships. One could see dry stream beds full of pebbles, whose banks looked like half-open lips that were parched and clamoring for water from the sky. Among these cliffs, there were large caves that were probably the lairs of wild animals that were hiding from the presence of man. One of our companions had peered into one of these caves and panicked at the sight of some green eyes shining back from inside. There were dozens of partridges that nested and took shelter there. There were also enormous rodents. A few of our companions claimed to have captured some and eaten them roasted.

That is how we spent our Sundays. On Monday, we returned to reality, the reality of forced labor. The bugle sounding reveille, formation, and the salute to the French flag, and then the departure of that group of men dressed in rags who marched sorrowfully along the dusty red path. A wretched army. They were all Spanish refugees. There were functionaries, doctors (I remember Dr. Rejón Delgado), industrialists, mechanics, and soldiers, even the handsome Pedrillo, from Palo de Málaga, who used to earn his living scaling fish for restaurants and fry shops. The sturdiest among us carried heavy sledge hammers to break boulders, others carried pitchforks, and some had shovels and wheelbarrows. The rest, like me, carried a truncheon. Everyone had his assigned place.

The Spanish consul in Oujda arrived even to this place, and had us line up in the courtyard. They say he told his compatriots, "Whoever wants to return to Spain can request it in writing right here, and I guarantee that nothing will happen to you. The worst that can happen to the most rebellious among you is that, instead of building a railroad for the French, you will do it for your own homeland. Whoever wants to leave here right now, take one step forward." There was booing and catcalls. No one stepped forward. They even insulted him. We all hoped to return, but not now. We would wait until the re-conquest of our country had begun.

The days passed slowly and bitterly. Thank goodness the four of us who lived in my tent were from the same region and we lived in the most absolute harmony because of the affinity of our ideas. In other tents, some had brought the flag of their army division from Spain to here. Loud acrimonious arguments could be heard between Socialists and Communists. Political passions had contributed to the fall of the Republic. While they persist, there will never be a re-conquest or reconciliation.

The French say that the peoples of the Iberian Peninsula have an explosive and rebellious mentality and temperament. For any futile motive, we go out into the street to sow disorder. That is why foreigners say we need a Salazar or a Franco to unite us by force for the good of the nation. No one wants to yield an inch of their convictions, and that brings ruin to us all.

The French don't think the way we do. They seek the most appropriate means to defend their private interests which, in the end, are the common interests of their country. They become Communists, Socialists or Republicans, atheists or Catholics according to what the circumstances demand. They established the Commune and carried out the storming of the Bastille to eliminate feudalism and the caste system. As the years passed, they formed other clans of the rich and the poor, but they have made twice the progress we have with their pragmatic democracy. How different from Spain! There the path taken by the rich is only for the rich, and the path taken by the poor is only for the poor.

Inauguration of the First Stretch of the Trans-Saharan

It is December now. We had already broken up enough cubic meters of rocks for this stretch of the rail bed. A locomotive was advancing with ties and rails. They were forced to work at a fast rate since the date of the inauguration of the Bouarfa-Kenadsa line had already been announced. All that remained was an uneven section to cut through for the train to pass. The whole company went there. There was no more need for truncheons. Only mattocks, shovels and wheelbarrows, and our brute force. Since that cut was not progressing as quickly as they had calculated, they brought a group of Arab boys, who worked alongside us. On that December day, with the two sections joined, the Bouarfa-Kenadsa line of the Trans-Saharan Railroad was completed. Our companion Antonio Iglesias, who was the company's butcher, was in charge of sacrificing several rams and ewes. There was to be an extraordinary feast.

When one of those who had been here almost two years would ask me what I thought of this situation, I always responded that I was only going to be here for the time it took to get my papers in order. My great friend,

Monsieur Mallein, was arranging my departure, as he told me in his letters. I was hoping that, one day or another, the orders I wanted would arrive. These lads were telling me that whoever had ended up here wouldn't be allowed to leave until the war ended. In spite of that, I trusted my luck, whether through Monsieur Mallein or through the captain in Oued Zea, who made me fill out some forms requesting passage to Mexico. Or perhaps the "Industrial Production and Labor" service in Rabat, which was our "master," would decide it didn't need us anymore once this section of the Trans-Saharan was finished. The fact is, I could already taste the possibility of departure.

The day of the inauguration arrived. They ordered us to wear our best clothes. We Spaniards thought it would be better to put on the most outlandish rags we could find. Our formation was located some two hundred meters from the tracks. They instructed us to cheer and applaud, just like in all demonstrations orchestrated by a dictatorship. A luxurious blue and white locomotive appeared, pulling several cars and bearing the name of the French explorer René Caillé. The coaches were full of people, whom we supposed were supporters of Marshall Pétain. We were supposed to shout, and each of us did our duty with pleasure, hollering the ugliest swearwords I have ever heard in my life. At least we got off our chests some of what we had pent up inside. Later, a fine meal and wine. It was the inauguration of the Trans-Saharan, constructed, forged, and, on occasion, dampened by the tears of Spanish expatriates.

I have been sent sardines, some of them canned and others salted and pressed. The salted and pressed sardines, known as *sardinas arenques*, are a food fit for the gods to our companions from Alicante. I remember 'Tonono,' from

Callosa del Segura, who used to beg me to give him some *arenques*, which he considered a succulent feast.

I have never been a glutton. With a piece of bread, I can spend a whole day without going hungry. I was satisfied with what I had and, if I wanted, I would buy some dates as sweet as honey from the desert nomads. They were very nutritious. What were eight hours of work to me? I was accustomed to putting in eighteen or twenty hours in the factory without sitting down. Sometimes, at dawn, after a night of continuous hustle and bustle, it would look like we were finished and could sleep for a few hours. Then a boat loaded with sardines would put into port and our work would start all over again. That really was a life of forced labor, of authentic slavery, even while enjoying total freedom. Working on the railroad, I actually gained weight since I had no worries of any kind. At the factory, I was always afraid some worker would fall asleep and his steam caldron would blow up, and this fear would often keep me awake for days on end. I no longer had to deal with those thousands of problems brought on by running a factory. And the dry climate, far from the sea's dampness, contributed to the disappearance of my throat infections. I breathed freely through bronchial tubes that had occasionally been a little delicate in the past.

I was the one who spent the most time writing and, consequently, I was also the one who received the most letters.

At the beginning of this diary, I told how, on July 18, 1936, the mayor of my town, Manuel Flores Rodríguez, came asking for men willing to take up arms to maintain order and protect the border. Later, he fled in a boat headed for Tangiers. Now, he is a few kilometers from here, in charge of a team of spike drivers who are laying tracks. During the war he was in Madrid, where he fought bravely until he received the order to retreat. There were some truck drivers headed for his camp and I gave them some packages of canned sardines to take to him. I also sent him the last address I had in Casablanca, in case fate should reunite us. My compatriot Miguel Gómez Barranco, 'Miguel, Bruna's son,' as we used to call him, is there too.

An Official Threat

When old Captain Brunikel would run into me, he would stop because he liked to chat with me in French. He had taken me for an intellectual or something of the sort. But there was a French officer of German descent who did not look kindly on my conversations with the Polish captain. I had already had several altercations with this officer when he was berating some worker and I would reproach him for it. He was tall and wore a long black cape, and so we used to call him 'Dracula.'

That day, after mealtime, I went to wash the dishes and spoons belonging to our tent, because it was my turn. I was engaged in this task when two Arab soldiers arrived on horseback. They were soldiers who kept an eye on the nomadic tribes on the edge of the desert. They dismounted and one of them asked me for water, which I gave to him in an aluminum pot while their horses drank from the trough next to the water tanks. The first Arab quenched his thirst and, when the second one took the pot, 'Dracula' arrived. He saw the Arab drinking and rushed furiously to his side and snatched the pot from him, shouting and gesticulating violently. The Arabs mounted their horses and left. Then 'Dracula' turned to me, rebuking me and threatening to send me to the disciplinary camp. There were many other workers there washing utensils. They gathered around and some of them confronted the officer, telling him that I was new and didn't know of the orders that prohibited the sharing of water with outsiders and that, furthermore, those who requested the water were armed soldiers. 'Dracula' continued shouting, "This one is going to the disciplinary camp."

I don't know who it was that notified Captain Brunikel, but he arrived and saw what was happening. "Have a little compassion for those who need help," he told the officer.

"Compassion for whom? For Arabs? For these men?" 'Dracula' said, pointing to us. "These men are from a defeated army. They are better off here than in their towns' cemeteries."

Those words stung my heart and filled me with rage. We were from a defeated army? I immediately thought of my beloved Spain and its sufferings. And seeing these men in rags, I couldn't control myself and began to shout, "A defeated army? No. A people's army that fought Franco's Moorish mercenaries, that fought the Portuguese 'Viriatos' and Italian Black Shirts and those sent by the Rumanian Cantacuzene, not to mention the German Condor Legion with its airplanes that strafed our highways and bombed our towns. We fought the other half of Spain, ruled by military men and priests, and we held out for almost three years! And you French allowed the Germans to occupy your country in two months! And you call us a defeated army?"

At that moment I felt a firm hand grasp me by the arm. It was Captain Brunikel, who took me, along with 'Dracula,' to his camp office. Since he knew the cause of the row, he did not want to take my side and infuriate the officer. But he intervened, saying that the camp regulations were strict and we must bear in mind that water was scarce and indispensable for our survival, but that there should be some elasticity in the regulations. He pointed out that I was new and unaware of that order, that the Arabs were soldiers just like us and were armed. When we left the Captain's "bureau" I thought to myself that if this had happened to any other of my poor compatriots, he would have been taken to the terrible disciplinary camp for harsh punishment.

By now, the disciplinary camp was a fortress built of great blocks of red clay mixed with dry grass that, after drying in the desert sun, the prisoners had to carry on their backs to the construction site, more than a kilometer away. The camp was surrounded by an area covered with lime and if anyone tried to cross it, the soldiers on guard duty opened fire. When, during the first days here, we spoke fearfully of that terrible disciplinary camp, I gave it little thought, saying that no one who worked hard would end up there. I never imagined that for the slightest confrontation, protest, or expression not to the liking of some bigwig, a poor refugee could be hauled off to that camp, no matter how good a worker he was. This officer, who tried to pass himself off as a Frenchman even though he was German, and who always needed to be the center of attention in his black cape, this 'Dracula' as we called him, had it out for me. An Andalusian I knew used to say he was the "black shadow" that followed workers everywhere.

After this incident, many of my companions told me to control my anger and maintain my serenity and patience as they had for nearly two years. They were resigned, bereft of all support, but since I had grown up unaccustomed to reprimands I couldn't bear being insulted.

Talking to Pedro Rodríguez, from Puebla de Guzmán, he told me about the time when a companion showed up limping with a wounded shin and saying he had been bitten by one of the many dogs owned by the nomads. This refugee was evacuated to the Pasteur Institute in Casablanca to receive treatment for rabies and the news spread rapidly from camp to camp. He was there in the big city for a short time, enjoying his semi-freedom until, by his calculations, they would come looking for him to take him back to the Trans-Saharan Company, at which time the man disappeared, hiding out in the Spanish district, and they never found him.

Soon after that, another refugee was also bitten by one of the nomads' dogs. These dogs were never located and such cases became more frequent. Eventually, the company officials began to suspect they were the victims of a stratagem these workers used to free themselves of the yoke of the concentration camps. They ordered a search and found tongs that had been fashioned to resemble a dog's jaw. Workers were using them to "bite" themselves. This shows how desperate the prisoners were to escape their situation of complete subjugation which never varied: lining up for roll call every morning and every evening, the raising and lowering of flags, salutes, and paramilitary regimentation. They could see no end to this living hell. There was also the case of one of the refugees who got hold of a camel and, provisioned with a sack of food, took off one night in the direction of the sea through a region where there was nothing but dunes that shifted with the wind. Nothing was ever heard of him again. Finding a man in that desert was like finding a needle in a haystack.

Departure

Christmas Eve was drawing near. We were lined up in formation when the interpreter read the orders from the "Industrial Production and Labor" service, which said, "every foreign worker with experience in the industry for canning fish or other foods, take one step forward." Neither shy nor lazy, I took two steps forward so they could see me well. After a brief consultation, the captain approached me and said, "Do you have documentary proof of your experience?"

"Sir, I have two certificates, one from the Algero-Marocain Company and another from Monsieur Mallein."

"*Bien, après formation apportez moi ces papiers.*"

There were loud murmurings throughout the formation. After we were dismissed, I found myself surrounded by everyone. Some of the men embraced me and several of them asked me to help them get out too.

I presented my work certificates and, the following day, I had an official letter from the "Industrial Production and Labor" service, along with a train ticket to Casablanca, where I had been arrested almost four months before. In the letter, I was granted fifteen days leave, after which I was to report to the Oued Akrouch Camp in Rabat for "duty assignment."

"You see, my dear companions," I told Antonio Iglesias, Pedro Rodríguez, and Antonio 'The Border Guard,' "I have my fairy godmother with me. I came here only long enough to be able to write an account of your life and what is going on here. Look, this is my passport to freedom."

There was a small party in my honor. We drank two bottles of anis from Algiers. We ate all the packages of dates and we exchanged many scraps of paper with the names and addresses of the family members of those who had to stay, we hoped for not much longer. Night was almost upon us when the Kenadsa-Bouarfa train came through with boxcars full of merchandise and horses, and all my companions came to say good-by.

The train only stopped for a few seconds. I threw my suitcase inside a car and had half my body inside and the other half hanging out when the train began to move. Someone shouted to the engineer but he didn't hear a thing. Suddenly, from inside the car, two men emerged, grabbed me by the arms and helped me in. What a fright it gave me! If I had fallen, the wheels would have ground up my legs right when I was about to regain my freedom. There in the car were two men with long beards and large worn-out suitcases. They were from the old Legion and were going to Bouarfa for medical exams. We stood in the boxcar and talked. They were of the same politics as me and hoped to get out of here soon. This stretch of the Trans-Saharan was already finished and they wondered what the Mediterranean-Niger Company would do now to maintain so many lines. "Maybe they will take us further inland to extend the line toward Dakar," one of them said.

"It isn't an easy route, but they could do it," I said. "The important thing is for someone to come and help us in the re-conquest of Spain. Then all this will seem to us as if it had only been a tragic nightmare."

Since they were more familiar than me with the customs of this area, I asked them to give me the name of some place where I could spend the night. They told me to ask for the bakery run by their companion Vega. He was from Asturias and was in charge of the bakery for Bouarfa's main camp. The train stopped in the Trans-Saharan capital. I went to the bakery, asked for Vega and, after showing him the documents releasing me from the camp, we chatted for an hour. Vega assigned me an old but good bed near the fire. The following day, there were procedures and paperwork at the Mediterranean-Niger Company's central headquarters, where I ran into my friend Rafael Villaplaza from Alicante. He told me that the Bouarfa-Oujda station was five kilometers distance. After that, I would take the Oujda-Casablanca line. By nightfall, I was in the Bouarfa railway station.

Until the train arrived, I was with some fellow Socialists, all refugees, from the station master to the last grease monkey. They had a central heating system they had installed themselves, and which was blazing in a formidable coal stove. The intense cold of the Saharan night could not be felt in that waiting room.

Seated on a bench, the station master told me that the first day they arrived in that place there was a terrible snowstorm that collapsed their tents. They spent the whole night shaking snow off the canvas. This place is on the buttresses of the Atlas Mountains, pummeled either by the "sirocco," or Saharan wind, with its unbearable heat, or by spectacular snowstorms.

I thanked them all for helping me. The following night, after almost twenty-four hours on the train, I arrived in Oujda on the Algerian border. Three times, the gendarmes asked for my papers and I showed them the ones provided me by the company. From this train, I transferred to the one from Casablanca, whose coaches were crammed with people of every race and color. The most common language was Spanish, but with an accent that almost made me laugh. It was spoken by the Algerian descendants of the Spanish Moors who had been expelled from Spain in 1492. They were going to spend the Christmas and New Year holidays in Casablanca. Family reunions. I was all alone but I couldn't complain. I was alive and that was enough.

Seated in the corridor on my inseparable suitcase with my back against the wooden seat, I was headed for Casablanca. Whenever I was about to doze off, I would recall that terrible night in the fish truck on my way to Lisbon. Every detail of that long night's journey, with all its consequences, had been etched in my mind forever. The Oujda-Casablanca train rolls on, stopping in every one of the cities whose jails I got to know when I traveled in the other direction. At dawn, we arrived in the economic capital of the kingdom.

At the Police Station

I presented my papers. They read them and looked at me as if I were some kind of odd duck. They stamped them and said, "You can spend those fifteen days at your ease wherever you like, but bear in mind that once your leave is up, if you do not report to the Oued Akrouch Camp near Rabat for 'duty assignment,' we will have to arrest you and send you to the disciplinary camp."

I spent that night with the Mallein family and, during our Christmas Eve dinner, we discussed how to deal with my situation. Monsieur Mallein had requested a technician in the canning industry from the "Industrial Production and Labor" service in Rabat, and was optimistic about the results of his negotiations. When my leave expired, I reported to the camp on the Oued Akrouch where it flows into the Regreg (Oued Bou Regreg: River of Frogs), where I found the same system in force as in the Trans-Saharan, the same worn-out coats handed down by the Legion, the same formations, the same raising and lowering of the flag to the accompaniment of bugles. The camp was run by German Jews who were hiding out in this French military organization. This camp was for convalescents, for refugees seeking passage to South America, and for workers who were to be rented out by the "Industrial Production and Labor" service. There were thirty or forty men there who should have embarked for the Argentine Republic, but their ship never arrived. Since the camp was on the confluence of two rivers, these men had given it the name "Shipwreck Island." We were about ten kilometers from where the Regreg flowed into the Atlantic.

I arrived in winter and torrential rains had caused the rivers to swell. Abundant firewood floated down the swollen rivers. Ramón Mundo, from Castellón de la Plana, kept himself busy with a huge grapple and rope with which he dragged tree trunks to the shore, keeping us well supplied with fuel for the kitchen. We slept on straw in the tents. Hundreds of fleas would crawl up our sleeves and the legs of our pants. Even if we covered ourselves well, they would also come in through our shirt collars. This torment was worse than the flies in Bouarfa. At least there we could sleep if we turned out the light. There were some of these refugees who could sleep despite the fleas, but I would spend the whole night scratching myself. I don't know how the refugees from Spain and other countries put up with the terrible fleabites day after day.

One day, I asked the camp directors if I could build a "chalet" surrounded by a moat. Since I planned to build it for four cots, I spoke to old Rogelio Piñero from Cartagena, Campanela from Alicante, and Cosaux from Orihuela. As always when I made up my mind to do something, I didn't think twice about it, but immediately took action. While some of us gathered rocks with a wheelbarrow, others brought red clay. We had a barrel with two hundred liters of water and, after digging a moat fifty centimeters deep, we proceeded to erect the walls, which were fifty centimeters thick. Every day, little by little, we raised the walls. Our companions from the other groups made fun of us. "These guys think they are going to be here the rest of their lives." It was necessary to put up with all their jests and keep my friends from giving up, in which case it would have been difficult for me to continue the project alone. I argued that it was a useful sacrifice we were making because even if we never got to use it, at least it would be there for those who came later from the desert.

Once we had built the walls to a height of two meters twenty centimeters, we proceeded to construct the roof. It consisted of sturdy poles of cork oak that formed an A, fastened solidly together with nails that Campanela made at the forge. We also found a cable from an old crane and frayed it over a fire. Its wires were invaluable to me for tying strong bundles of reeds with which we covered the whole roof. I worked tirelessly to spur on my helpers. Campanela sawed branches from wild olive trees and cork oaks and built four cots on tall legs. The rectangular beds held a metal screen which would support our future mattresses. Every afternoon, legionnaires and our Spanish friends would come to watch me lashing the reeds to the roof at just the right incline so that not even a single drop of water would accumulate there.

At the time, a bridge was being built over the Akrouch River. The overseer for the project was a Portuguese friend of mine, named Ferrero. I asked him to let me sweep out the bin where the cement powder was stored when it stood empty waiting for a new truckload. In this way, every two or three days I was able to sweep up two or three sacks of cement, which were of great use to me. I added coarse sand from the river to the cement mix, which I deposited first on the peak of the roof and then worked downward little by little. The cement took hold on the reeds and wire ties and formed such a solid roof that I have to laugh as I recall what such a group of spontaneous builders were able to accomplish. The windows and doors were similarly fashioned from bundles of reeds which, cut in half and retied with wires, were almost as solid as a wooden door.

Near the entrance to our "chalet," my friend Rogelio Piñero, the oldest of us four, built shelves, just like in a library, and stocked them with books by the most famous philosophers from all of human history down to the present time.

The Housewarming Party

The captain of the camp telephoned the "Industrial Production and Labor" service in Rabat and bigwigs, along with some small fry, came out from that capital to celebrate our feat. They all had flattering things to say to us and asked the others to follow our example. We were fêted with tortillas, each made with forty fresh Picabuey eggs.[23] We also received a double ration of wine. I had given three coats of whitewash to the roof in order to close any pores there might have been in that pyramid. Then we built a bonfire of straw and grass to kill the fleas in our blankets and bedclothes, and arranged them on the high cots we had built. How well we slept after that! Later, when torrential rainfalls arrived, not a single drop penetrated our "chalet." Meanwhile, in the other barrack huts built of red clay, with roofs of the same material, they had to spend the night standing, for fear the whole adobe structure would collapse.

When the sun returned, the whole camp would revive. The Italian and German ex-legionnaires operated a sort of aviary with hundreds of ducks and chickens. Men

---

[23] According to a note in the manuscript by the author himself, this bird also goes by the name *Aguijabuey*. It is a small bird resembling a stork: *Ardeola Ibis*.

from Alicante and Murcia had a workshop where they made shoes, braiding hemp fibers and sewing them with large needles to make the sole, and fashioning the uppers out of the recycled tatters of legionnaire uniforms. Another group spent its time cutting reeds that grew on an island in the middle of the Regreg River.

One day, several companions arrived from Bouarfa. They were convalescing from a typhus epidemic that had swept through the country, affecting even the Trans-Saharan capital. The news they brought us from the desert was that, having completed that stretch of railroad, panic had spread among our companions, because it was rumored that the workers' brigades were going to be transferred to the interior to build another line to Dakar. The reports I received from friends in Rabat were just the opposite. They said that the "Industrial Production and Labor" service was trying to find jobs for these hundreds of foreigners, renting them out to private enterprises in order to solve the immense problem of so many mouths to feed.

I wrote Monsieur Mallein asking him to contact the owners of canning factories to see if they would contract the former mayor of Ayamonte and Miguel Gómez Barranco, my two compatriots, whom I hoped to have the opportunity to see again. According to custom, they would have to come to this camp for "duty assignment." A week later, the camp captain came to tell me that the two people I had asked to be incorporated here would be arriving today. I leaped with joy at this news which filled me with delight. Within a few hours I would have them by my side.

That mayor, a self-taught man from a working-class family and a cooper by trade, had educated himself and acquired a solid cultural foundation with the many books he had read and assimilated. He was a graduate of the great "university of the common man," and that is why we elected him to that high municipal post. Running a town is not an easy thing to do. Especially those in Andalusia, full of modern revolutionary ideas that conflicted with the religious spirit handed down to the older generations by the archaic and traditional Spain. They were two worlds, distinct and at odds, that fractured the national consensus. There was no possible ground for compromise between a religious fanatic ready to die and kill for a hypothetical but unknown God, and a young left-wing idealist who only saw value in the strength of his hands and the benefits of science, and for whom death was nothing but a reconversion into matter.

The religious fanatics were the minority, but they had the most power. They had money, laws, a caste system, and the military on their side. The others, the majority of Spaniards, were the idealistic but defenseless youth, without capital, without the protection of the law, and without arms to defend themselves. That was the political climate in which Manolo Flores exercised authority. It was difficult, but I was pleased with the way he used to run the Town Council meetings, leaving everyone in attendance satisfied. I often remember that moment on July 18 when he announced, "I need forty willing men. I will arm them to maintain order and protect the border with Portugal." That was the moment this story began. In the wee hours of the morning of July 29, 1936, with the rebel troops approaching and sensing danger from Salazar's Portuguese dictatorship, he embarked with his companions from Huelva, from the president of the provincial government, Don Juan Tirado Figueroa, to Elías Palma Ortega, who was one of the leaders of the regional Freemasons.[24] Manolo Flores later arrived in Tangiers and from there made his way to the Republican zone, where he joined the army and fought on the Madrid front until the last moment.

We were to be reunited at last. It seemed as though I was trembling with emotion. What an urge I had to tell him, "You left me in the hands of the enemy and fled." But no. It was all in the past now. I am alive and I owe my life to my own efforts, my cunning, and my luck. The best course is to remain silent. The thing happened the way it did. It was an oversight caused by the haste of escape, and an oversight can be forgiven.

---

24 A native of Ayamonte and sales representative of the publishing house Casa Alfa, Palma Ortega was a follower of Diego Martínez Barrio. He held high offices in the labor movement. After intervening actively during the days following the military coup, he fled the city in one of the boats that departed for North Africa.

The Arrival of the Mayor of Ayamonte

For more than an hour I had been waiting on the highway at the entrance to the camp. Finally, the covered cart that brings mail, supplies, and food from Rabat arrived. That day, it also brought Miguel Barranco and Manolo Flores. When they got off the cart, it was almost noon. We embraced and exchanged greetings. I made them an extraordinary meal of fresh river fish, fried in a batter the German cook had prepared that morning after I paid him a few francs.

After eating, we had ourselves photographed to commemorate the occasion. The whole time, Flores besieged me with questions. He was impatient, thirsty to know what had happened to the town and to his family during his absence. We went for a walk along the river's edge, conversing endlessly. Night fell and my mates at the "chalet" allowed them to come in and sit on the edge of my cot. Some fell asleep and others listened attentively to our conversation, until the moment arrived to tell Flores about the imaginary lists the Fascists said they had found in the city hall with the names of the people we were going to kill. The news was a rude blow to the former mayor.

He slapped his forehead, turned pale, and shouted, "What rabble! What scoundrels! We who have been the greatest 'Don Quixotes' Spain has ever known throughout its entire history. We who have pardoned everyone, from General Sanjurjo to the last Fascist criminal. When all we did was arrest, with respect and under orders from the governing authorities, those individuals who were in danger when those others came from the mines to take out their rage on them—and these beasts repay our kindness shooting innocent women and men. We who took in and protected the children and wives of civil guards, knowing that many of them had betrayed the Republic." Manolo Flores was suffering immensely. "They perpetrate these horrendous crimes against us, killing so many poor devils and leaving them scattered about the countryside. And for what? For what?" he said, almost shouting. "Where is God? Where is this impotent God? If I had another hundred years, I would live them without forgiving those people ever. Now there is no way I will be able to sleep tonight. Tomorrow, I am going to ask them to send me back to Spain. That's right! I have to go to my town and shout that this story about the lists is an infamy, an enormous outrage. Then, if they want, let them kill me."

Miguel Gómez Barranco and I tried to calm him down. He was pretty worked up. I told him, "Go back to Spain? What do you know about what is happening there? You would be killed the moment you set foot on Spanish soil, with no benefit to our cause. We must wait. We must be patient. That is the greatest virtue for a fighter. That is what gives him the power to triumph."

In the wan light of the oil lamp, Manolo's face had a greenish hue. An occasional indiscreet tear fell from his eyes. I had never before seen him as depressed as at that moment. The lists, the famous lists that they had invented, had turned up in all the towns of Andalusia so they could prove "the evil intentions of the reds," a pretext for shooting so many thousands of workers. The truth had appeared in the Huelva newspaper *Odiel*, which had proclaimed, "Our tactic should be the same as the one we employed in North Africa, the tactic by which we execute five percent of the population, leaving the remainder so paralyzed by terror that they will never rise up against us."

Our conversation that night came to a close. Manolo said, "I am tired. I have protected presumed enemies in the name of humanitarian laws and in the name of the nobility of a town that never knew what crime was, and that town, my town, has been drenched in blood by a treacherous band of. . ."

". . .of prowling beasts," I added. My compatriots left our "chalet." That night they were going to sleep in a tent on the straw of "purgatory," as some called it.

The bugle played its florid reveille. Formation. The counting off of the prisoners. Salutes to the French flag as it was raised up the pole. There was no forced labor here. After making our beds and sweeping our floor, we went to the refectory and had breakfast.

After that, most of us went fishing. Using the old mosquito netting from a window, I had fashioned a drag net with which I caught more than a kilo of shrimp each day. Cooked with a little salt and accompanied by a glass of beer, this was our daily treat.

On Sundays, Manolo Flores and Miguel Gómez always came to my "site," as I called my shrimping operation, and we would spend the day in pleasant conversation.

It did not take long for my assignment orders to arrive. I had been "rented" to my friend Monsieur Mallein, just as we had agreed. I still have the famous contract, a document drawn up in the middle of the twentieth century, which contains words threatening arrest and imprisonment in the disciplinary camps in the event of my escape, which my "owner" was obliged to report to the police within twenty-four hours. With my suitcase stuffed with more papers than clothing, I walked out to the cart which would take me to Rabat. There were my dear friends and my collaborators in the construction of the "chalet," of which I have left my cot and my place to Manolo Flores. Everyone asks me to remember them and to do what I can to get them out.

I arrived in Rabat and from there I took the train to Mehedia. That is where the *Carranza almadraba*, or tuna fishery, was located. The manager of the operation was my great compatriot Manuel Montes Cumplido. He lived in Mehedia (Kenitra), and took it upon himself to recruit personnel from Ayamonte, who were experts in the industry.

I was eating with Manuel Montes and his family when there was a knock on the door. They told me there was a person who was anxious to see me. I went out to receive him. What a surprise and great joy it was for me to see Jesús Feria, 'Cross eyes' as we used to call him, one of the few who escaped the massacres. Jesús was one of those who were with me until the last moment. He was later arrested and, while in prison, was tortured by being whipped until they had to pick out the pieces of his shirt that were encrusted in his flesh. They applied salt and vinegar to his back as a cure. Here, for the first time, I heard the hair-raising recital of horrors that would never be forgotten by those who managed to survive them. It was the terrifying tale of knocks on cell doors in the pre-dawn hours when a horrific silence accompanied the reading of names, the names of those who would be "saved" from their dreadful imprisonment by being assassinated.

I was comforting Jesús and promised him that justice would be done. Many other compatriots of both sexes arrived, anxious to see me five years after my famous escape. They all congratulated me for having survived and told me how happy they were to receive my letter from Casablanca announcing my arrival in that Moroccan capital. It had been a day of general celebration. I told them all that Manolo Flores and Miguel Gómez Barranco were in good health and would soon begin to work. After saying good-by to everyone, I went to the Kenitra station and took the train to Rabat, where I had to sign some papers for the "Industrial Production and Labor" service.

The newspapers continue announcing that the Germans, Italians, and Japanese are reaping victory after victory, and we refugees are crestfallen, since these developments were contrary to our interests. But we never gave up hope for the triumph of our democratic ideals.

After Rabat, I went again to the central police station in Casablanca to legalize my work contract and obtain my safe-conduct pass so I could go to the fishing town of Safi, located like an eagle's nest on a cliff overlooking the Atlantic. There was a factory belonging to a French family which had closed when the owner died. Monsieur Mallein told me that I had to get it up and working in the shortest time possible. I presented my documents at the Safi police station. There they made me a provisional residency card which would allow me complete liberty to move about and feel at home at the counters of the bars and cafés. There were more than fifteen hundred Portuguese and two hundred Spaniards living in Safi. The latter worked on the sardine boats. Almost all of them were ship mechanics and, for the most part, were from the north of Spain. The sardine industry dominated the economy to such an extent that the Safi postmark said, "Sardine Capital of the World."

I was living at the Hotel Sevillana, which was indeed the property of a woman from Seville, María Molina, who had been a singer of the popular songs known as *tonadillas*. I have no idea how or when she came to Safi and established herself here. She was very helpful and treated me like a member of the family. I told her how, during the bus ride to Safi, we stopped in every town and French gendarmes entered the bus asking for papers. When they got to me and read my safe-conduct pass, they looked at me as if I were a dangerous bandit. It was totally the opposite of what always used to be the pleasant and gallant spirit of France. They were provocateurs and supporters of Pétain, who had accommodated the Germans and was now governing the French nation.

Once I was established at the hotel, I decided I was honor bound to bring my fiancée here. At the house of my friend Montes, from Kenitra, and in the presence of his daughters Paquita, Pilar, and Adela, I asked them to do what they could to get her a work contract so she could join me. Later, I would make arrangements to marry her and legalize our situation. I wrote her a fairly extensive letter giving her an account of my life.

I Become Productive Again

I was full of youth and energy. In two weeks, the factory was up and running with one hundred and fifty women and fifteen men as workers. During the first days, the factory was visited by police agents, who ordered cooking oil or canned sardines. One fine day, a certain Manuel López, police commissioner of the Port of Safi, showed up. He was an ancient combatant from the French army and had been born in Algeria. He spoke Spanish as well as I did. Together, with a good bottle of vintage wine, we spoke of the Spanish problem and I took advantage of the opportunity to tell him everything that was in the "Diary" I had written, without hiding anything.

From that day on, I could count on friends in the police force. Some of them would tell me, "Don't blame us for the things that are happening. It is the German commission that gives the orders."

A month later, Flores and Barranco left the camp near Rabat and traveled to Agadir. They had been contracted to work in some friends' factories, where they would have to prove their worth. We were able to make contact by telephone and exchange our first greetings.

Since the hotel, where I was living in room six, was some three kilometers from the factory, and work often ended in the wee hours of the morning, I had to walk that distance along a trace of desert highway on the edge of a cliff that was eighteen meters above the sea. Due to the wartime blackout and the lawlessness of the country, the trip involved a certain amount of danger and I decided to take over a plot on the factory grounds and build myself a small house with two rooms and a kitchen. I began to raise rabbits and chickens, and was living as well as I could within the limits of my demanding job. From among the personnel working at the factory, I picked out a little Moorish girl about eighteen years old, and assigned her the tasks of caring for my house and going to the market to buy what I needed for my meals. So, everything was sailing along smoothly, until one night. . .

The Landing of the Americans

It was November 8, 1942. It must have been about three o'clock in the morning of that day when I was awakened by the barking of a German shepherd I had been given. I opened a large folding knife from Albacete that I kept for self-defense and, with firm resolve, went out the door and took up a position in the dark on the coastal highway next to the factory entrance. I heard talking and listened intently. It was two Arab soldiers who were guarding the train tracks that passed behind my house. They were terrified. They told me that two black foreigners had caught them by surprise and taken their arms. I took them into the factory's patio and made them sit in a corner near the office. Three soldiers with a machine gun, a tripod, and a box, which I imagined contained ammunition, took up a position in the middle of the highway ten meters from the entrance to the factory. I approached the fence and, at that precise moment, an extraordinary light illuminated the whole town of Safi, revealing my presence. One of the soldiers aimed his rifle at me and asked in English, "Who are you?"

I answered, also in English, "I am a Spanish political refugee."

Imagine my surprise when the soldier replied, "*De verdad es usted español?*," but speaking in a Spanish that had a Central or South American lilt to it. It all became clear to me when he said, still speaking in my language, "I am Chico. I was born in Texas, but at home and in the street, we spoke Spanish."

"*Qué pasa?*" I asked.

"We have come to liberate the peoples of Europe from Fascism."

"*Hombre*," I said, "you don't know how happy I am to see you. With you here, I am closer to Spain."

Within a quarter hour there was a group of more than twenty brown-skinned young men. They were all natives of Puerto Rico and other lands that once belonged to us. An officer who also spoke Spanish arrived and asked me what those buildings were for. I explained that they were a sardine cannery owned by the French. The leader continued the interrogation, asking me if there were arms or artillery in the area. I pointed out an emplacement with two long-range cannons located two hundred meters behind my house. They were there to defend the Safi harbor. I also showed him where the legionnaires' barracks was. I told him they were all Spaniards and that he should not attack them. I explained to him that they would surrender without firing a shot, because they would be in favor of this landing by people who were Spain's friends. A simple conversation was all it took. At the time, the legionnaires were all in the barracks asleep.

"Are there lions around here?" one of the Americans asked me.

"*Hombre*, in the Casablanca Zoo there is a pair of them, but they are very old by now," I answered.

The day was beginning to break. In the pre-dawn light, I could make out two hundred ships on the sea. From some of them, airplanes took off and headed for Marrakech, the region's capital. The men gave me packets of coffee and tobacco and canned peaches in syrup. They had brought everything that was scarce here during the war. Chico, Luis Dones, Roldán, they all treated me with affection. The Arab soldiers were silent in their corner.

"Don't worry, everything will be alright," I told them.

Then I gave them a chicken to kill and pluck, since I planned to prepare everyone a magnificent breakfast. Here was what I had been hoping for. Long live beautiful liberty! These men will defeat the Fascists and hand me my Spain on a silver platter, the Spain that had been stolen from me. France would be free and England's freedom would be assured and, since these two countries were friends of the Spanish Republic, they would help us in the re-conquest. I am full of happiness. I feel like singing in honor of the imminent victory.

From other ships, scores of amphibious vehicles emerged, with their menacing machine guns. Once their wheels touched terra firma, they were put in gear and headed into the town. The French port captain tried to offer resistance to the landing with a small team of soldiers of the same nationality, but they fell immediately to the American machine guns. The two hundred sardine boats from Safi did not put out to sea and, consequently, the factory was closed for the day. The girl who worked in my house has arrived in a state of alarm to ask me what was going on. While she tidied up the house, I explained to her what that landing represented for me. I don't know if she understood what

I told her, but she seemed to feel safe in my house. Two blasts were heard from the French cannons located behind the house and we were all startled. The ships responded immediately. Projectiles from the American ships whistled over our roof.

I set to work with a pickax, and the little Moorish girl with a shovel. We dug a trench in the patio and covered it with a large cart for transporting sardines from the Port. Abouch, as the girl was named, trembled with fear. She wanted to run away, but I restrained her until calm was restored. It was eleven o'clock in the morning. The cannons were captured by the Americans and the machine guns fell silent.

Abouch took off and ran into the countryside. I knew her family lived twelve kilometers away, but she was young and could reach home in less than an hour. I emerged from my trench with a great desire to investigate and find out what was going on. By then, the two Arab soldiers had left. I fed my chickens and rabbits and, after a rather late breakfast due to the circumstances, I let my dog loose and closed the wrought-iron gate to my patio. I took the highway and headed for town. I passed shell fragments that shined like silver and must have weighed more than half a kilo. The highway was full of fugitives who were fleeing to the countryside. There were women, men, and children, each one carrying whatever they could, straw mats, blankets, boxes, baskets. I kept walking and remembering all I had seen. When I got to the main street, all one could see were jeeps and American soldiers. The members of the Jewish community were cheering from the balconies of their houses, drinking champagne and offering it to the other Europeans and the soldiers.

There I found out that the legionnaires had given up without firing a shot and had been taken as prisoners to one of the large ships anchored in the bay. I was relieved. I had been afraid for them because they were all Spanish political refugees who were forced by circumstances to enlist in the Legion. Like me, they too had heard the terrible phrase that we would never forget, "The cemetery of your home town, the Legion, or a concentration camp." And between being shot or sent to a concentration camp, the best choice was to enroll in the Legion where, if you save your skin, you can count yourself among the survivors, and they all wanted to live because they were so young. I knew almost all these legionnaires. Whenever they entered some café where I was, I always bought a round, since they usually lacked the economic means to have a few drinks.

I continued on into the center of the town, observing everything and apprising myself of all the details concerning the landing. At that moment, carts pulled by mules went by, transporting the dead and wounded up the hill toward the hospital. There were few people out in the streets. The American jeeps patrolled the city center, driving fast in all directions. I went from house to house, visiting my fellow refugees and advising them to leave town in case Pétain's French bombed this dangerous bridgehead established by their enemies. My proposal was accepted and, by the time night fell, there was a large group of refugees at my house. They had brought all the food they could find. The more prudent among them had brought blankets so they could cover themselves at night. There were still some lingerers approaching along the highway when a French bomber passed overhead, nearly touching the roof of my house. It headed in the direction of the Port and dropped a bomb on one of the warehouses, causing deaths and injuries. The plane was shot down. While these circumstances persisted, no boats set out to fish and, consequently, there was no work to do at the canneries. We would have to make do with my chickens, which could feed us for a few days, and with vegetables from a farm about one hundred meters away that belonged to an old Portuguese woman, Señora Baptista.

Before it was dark, Pepe Ruiz, from Tangiers, went to see a French friend who lived a couple of kilometers away and raised pigs. By the time Pepe returned, night had already fallen and we were quite worried for his safety. He was sweating and breathing heavily from the effort of pulling along a pig he had bought. When we saw him with the recalcitrant animal, we broke into laughter and jests. "We are invincible," shouted Mariano Celaya, from Santander. That night, we dined and drank sumptuously. It was the first night we could celebrate our freedom after many years in which, to one degree or another, we all lived with the fear of being returned to Spain. It was a terror caused by Franco's friendship with Pétain, who might use us to ingratiate himself with the Spanish dictator. It had already happened to the most prominent Spanish refugees in France. Don Julián Zugazagoitia, the director of the newspaper *The Socialist*, Don Luis Companys, president of the Catalonian Generalitat, and many others no less distinguished, had been handed over to be shot in Spain. That medieval, Catholic, and traditionalist Spain, which was no Spain of ours.

Each one of us had a memory of the beloved little corner of Spain where we were born. We spoke of the public rallies we had attended and of our labor unions. And there were tributes to our inspirational leader Francisco

Largo Caballero. Among us, there were representatives of every region of Spain. We spoke a great deal about the Americans, in whom we had a blind faith, believing they would help us take back our country. We thought it would happen quickly. In a few months, we would be home. The Americans kept saying, "We came to liberate the people from the Fascist yoke." Each of us would be able to embrace our children, our mother, and our brothers. So many illusions. All these friends and comrades with me there who had saved themselves from the concentration camps because they were people of the sea. Most of them were ship mechanics who earned a good living. That night, Dr. Argimiro Galván spent a few hours with us. He was a native of Zamora, a political refugee who had established himself in Safi and was well-respected. We were sorry when he had to leave because he had to be on duty in case he was needed.

We were together almost three days, free to listen without fear to the radio broadcasts of the Allies which, day by day, were more encouraging. On the third day, the order came for the boats to go out fishing so the canning industry could resume operations. Everyone obeyed, but with a certain amount of fear that German submarines could sow the narrow entrance to the Safi Port with mines.

I received a communiqué by telephone from the police headquarters telling me to report there because they needed to talk to me. I went. Everyone received me enthusiastically. "You are now a free man," the commissioner told me. "You no longer have to report to these headquarters every month. With the American landing, everything has changed."

I smiled and thanked him, but inside I was seething with rage because these same police officers had served

Pétain and had persecuted us Spanish refugees as if we were criminals. Now they have changed their stripes, as the saying goes. I would have liked to tell them, "I have always been and always will be a free man until death. I was free in Spain and I was free in Portugal. One thing is the appearance of liberty, and another is the freedom one forges and maintains in one's heart."

I left police headquarters and ran into a group of legionnaires. They were overjoyed. The Americans had held them for only a short time on the ship. They told me of the continuous binges they had had. They say they have never been as well off as on that ship, where there was an abundance of whiskey. "It makes you want to cry," one of them said. "And now what? What are we going to do? Who will maintain us? We must find a solution to all of this." I advised them to reoccupy their barracks where they had good beds and a well-stocked pantry. While they had the means to survive, they should hold on until a solution arrived. Most of them decided to go to Casablanca, where they could find a way to get by in "refugeeland." There were two of them from Cabra who were construction workers. I told them I could find them jobs with Gallar, who was a building contractor.

One contingent remained in the Safi barracks and I often ran into them. After a little time passed, those who went to Casablanca and those who stayed in Safi reenlisted in the Legion, but this time on the side of freedom. They went to fight the German troops who had invaded part of North Africa. These legionnaires had been born in the land of Don Quixote and, consequently, they were ready to give their lives for liberty. Hadn't Don Quixote said, "The most precious gift on earth is liberty, and for it and for the woman one loves, my friend Sancho, one can give up one's life, because liberty is more valuable than all the treasures contained on the earth and in the sea"?

My American Guests

Almost every day I was visited by some American soldiers and officers of Hispanic descent. They told me they had been educated in schools where English was spoken, but in the cafés, during their street games, and at home, they continued speaking Spanish as their ancestors had done. They brought me gifts: American cigarettes and coffee, which I had gone without for so long. There were natives of Puerto Rico and Texas. We soon struck up a great friendship. I went out with them several times on their amphibious launches. I especially remember one Sunday when I invited them to a succulent meal of fresh sardines roasted over a charcoal fire. To accompany the sardines, I prepared a *piriñaca*, as we used to call it. It was a salad of finely chopped cucumbers, green peppers, onions, and tomatoes, seasoned with oregano and coarse salt, to be eaten with a spoon. Sardines and *piriñaca* washed down with a fine wine I had bought, a liter for each guest. Some of them sweetened their wine with sugar. One of them, Luis Dones, told me it was a meal fit for the gods.

Since my house had become the Safi headquarters of the Spanish Refugee's Association, other friends arrived, like Manolo Francés with his guitar, Mariano Celaya, who brought six lobsters, and Ventura Bazarra, who contributed a succulent and monumental Galician fish pasty. Ventura and his brother Gabriel were from Puebla de Caramiñal, *A Pobra do Caramiñal* in the Galician language. Pepe, from Tangiers, had decorated the locale with garlands of blood sausages and chorizos. The event was extravagant, an escape from everyday reality. The singing was started off by the Basques.

But not everything was a party. All those people were from the working world and spent nights on end without sleep, toiling in the sardine fishing industry, with daily visits to the Port's bar to help Spaniards who wanted to escape from the tyranny of Franco. Many were from the north of Spain and arrived on merchant ships, usually to take on a cargo of phosphates. Whoever wanted to go into exile was brought to my house and hid out there until their ship left port. Each of them told of the atrocities they had lived through in that hell. After a few days, I would put them in contact with our companions who drove trucks between Safi and Casablanca, either Rafael González, from Alicante, or Pepe Carretero, from Tangiers, who was employed by the Public Works Department. These drivers would take them to our organizations in Casablanca. There, in that great cosmopolitan city, they would apply for papers and many of them found work.

One day, a young man from Santander, one of those we had "rescued," was in Casablanca having a few drinks with a policeman, an Algerian who had acquired French nationality. The young man, thinking the policeman was just another refugee, told him there was an organization in the Port of Safi, which was headquartered in my house.

He even gave him the name of the driver who had brought him to Casablanca. By this inadvertent act, we were all discovered. The Casablanca police commission opened an investigation and sent a report dressing down the Safi police force. I was ordered to report and, this time, I wasn't received as a friend.

They told me, "We have regarded you as one of our best collaborators but, today, we are not going to forgive you for the dirty trick you have played on us. The commission accuses us of not being vigilant and of allowing dozens of fugitives from Spain to enter the country through our Port. This can bring severe consequences, including my dismissal. You, Señor Domínguez, do not understand the harm you have caused us with these clandestine activities. You should have notified us and we would have acted within the strictest legality. Now I have no other recourse but to arrest you. You even run the risk of being deported."

His last words filled me with dread. Deported?

"Señor commissioner," I said, "put yourself in my place as a political refugee. Would you betray a man who is trying to make a life for himself? Would you hand him over to the police without knowing what would become of that anguished fugitive?"

He didn't answer me. He gave a sign and another policeman took me to a cell. Since I had already been in so many predicaments and up so many dead-end streets, this arrest did not bother me as much.

I was thinking about the little Moorish girl in my house, about my dog that would have nothing to eat, my chickens, the ship I had contracted to bring in sardines, and my workers who would be out of a job.

They came for me in my cell and sat me down with an employee who typed my declaration. "I had a chance encounter in the Port with a compatriot and invited him to eat at my house without knowing he was in hiding. He asked me to seek out a companion who could take him to Casablanca because he didn't have the money for the trip, so I arranged it for him. This business about an organization to liberate possible refugees is like a journalist's fantasy."

Seated on a wooden bench with my shoulders against the damp wall of my cell, I pondered the situation I found myself in. It seemed to me I had only done my duty. The whole problem was caused by that young man, a compatriot who was seeking asylum. I couldn't denounce him to the police, because if the police arrested him and returned him to Spain, like the Portuguese did with Don Nicolás de Pablo, he would have been shot, whether he was a "red" or not. He would have been shot simply because he had tried to escape.

I was trying to fall asleep, but hunger pangs would not allow it. Just then, the cell door opened. I found myself facing Dr. Galván and my friend Luis Dones, the American sergeant, who had come to find out what had happened to me. The news of my arrest had spread through the town like wildfire. They had brought me a basket of food from a nearby restaurant.

"Doctor," I said, "thank you for this gesture. If they deport me, let it be to anywhere but Spain. I know how to earn a living."

Luis told me he had come to invite me to a meeting with the American commander of the garrison and had encountered this surprise. "You've been lucky," he said. "If it hadn't been for our invasion, they would have done whatever they wanted with you. Now, my superiors have already paid the commissioner a visit and you will be freed immediately."

The commissioner arrived and, after saying he had fulfilled his duty, gave the order for my release. At the door of the police headquarters there were about two hundred people, most of them Spaniards and Portuguese, but also Moroccans who worked for me. They had brought their families. I walked out, flanked by Dr. Galván and Luis Dones, and was greeted by applause, which filled me with emotion.

It was the middle of 1943. That night, I wrote again to my fiancée, telling her that a man's solitude is a bad counselor. I could no longer go on alone. Almost all the refugees' wives had joined them here, accompanied by their children. Some had documents and others had the courage to cross the sea on fishing boats. Many days went by without a reply. Then I wrote to Doña Dolores Gómez, the midwife. She did answer me, but her letter stung me to the core: "Don't wait for your fiancée. She is no longer interested in you. I have spoken to her and she has told me that she is not going to join you. Look for someone else and marry her."

Filled with pain, I asked myself, "What is going on here? How is it possible after all that has happened, and with this life of mine that they have saved? Something serious must have occurred." I sent her money with some fishermen who were on their way to Algeciras and a letter with instructions and the address of a family from there who would make arrangements for her to join me here, where our marriage would be recorded in the French Civil Registry. Finally, I received a letter in her handwriting. It was a renunciation of our entire past. She would not join me and, furthermore, she told me not to write her again. At that point, everything that had represented my youth and my dreams for the future was shattered. Why should I go on fighting for the re-conquest of Spain?

As the days passed, I was my old self again. We formed a commission to visit the American commander of the garrison. Our intention was to ask for help in the organization of a movement to take back our country. I was to be the spokesman who would set forth our wishes.

The Meeting with the Americans

"They tell me, Señor Domínguez, that you wanted to chat with me for a few minutes," the commander began, in correct Spanish. "Be aware that this is a private meeting. It is not official. The American viewpoint is that the Spanish Republic was kept going by bolshevism. You will understand that there was nothing we could do to help. It was the Communists who were making all the decisions. They were infiltrating every organism of power in the Republic. You refugees have to realize that the USSR is a one-party dictatorship which cannot be counted among the free and democratic nations of the world. For that reason, we have all decided to accept the lesser evil of Franco and his government so your country doesn't fall into the Russian sphere. This does not mean that if the Spanish people decided some day to change their regime and establish a genuinely democratic system, we wouldn't be there to help."

"That has been the guiding principal of the Fascists," I told him. "Their regimes were founded on anti-Communism. And more than six hundred thousand of us exiles in all parts of the world are the ones who are paying the price."

"Please, understand," he replied, "that the wounds are still fresh and your sudden return would bring in its wake a terrible settling of scores. There would be people hung in all the public squares of every town in Spain. Barely six years have transpired."

"So you Americans, the messengers of liberty, are condemning us to exile because we loved that liberty the same as you?" I said.

"I am very sorry. For now, we are fighting only to liberate Italy, Germany, and Japan from those totalitarian regimes. Afterwards, in due course, we will see."

We were offered some whiskey and sodas and departed with our hearts shattered. We were condemned to exile without knowing for how long and, meanwhile, in Spain the bugles would go on playing their song of extermination.

The following Sunday I held a meeting at my house for all the refugees. It was eleven o'clock in the morning and almost everyone in "refugeeland" was there. I gave an account of my private meeting with the Americans and described the opinion they had of us. There were some at the meeting who couldn't hold back their tears and others who shouted, "Traitors!" We now had to face reality. The truth of our situation was clear. We would each have to fend for ourselves.

Pepillo Carretero, born in the Bueyes marketplace in Tangiers, had fought in the war as a volunteer and spoke of his impressions of Spain. "Let's suppose," he said, "that our country is a huge milk cow and Doña María's children feed themselves at its teats. This aristocratic woman was a widow with a stupendous pension she collected following the death of her husband, who had been a general. Two of her brothers had high positions in the government and another was a bishop. She had two sons, little Javier and Alfonso. The former was an officer in the navy and the other presided over a high court of law. The whole family lives as it had always lived, feeding on the famous milk cow, which everyone said was the exclusive property of Doña María, both before and since her grandfathers gave up their high posts in the Philippines. Where was I going with all this?" Pepillo went on, "The rest of us Spaniards sow and toil to maintain the cow that feeds Doña María's children. Who, in this great noblewoman's family, was not born under a lucky star? Each of them, cousins, nephews, and grandchildren, even the ones who turn out to be as ignorant as a cork oak, is provided for by the whole kit and caboodle. Some close relative will always take charge of finding him a position so he can keep sucking on the teats of the generous Spanish cow for the rest of his life. And the rest of us? Up and at 'em. It's off to work so the world will go on being what they say it always was and should be. That is what it means to carry on tradition, a tradition that represents the past. Even when that past is dead. You can beat your brains out studying, building, creating, or planning enterprises to move the nation forward, but if you don't belong to Doña María's clan, you might as well die in obscurity, in anonymity, in abject poverty, because no one is going to give you a leg up. There's no room in the club for more members and, seeing I would never get a taste of the Spanish cow's teats, I had to go over to the other side."

    The next to speak was a refugee from Rentería. His Basque nationalist fervor was so great that he tried to instill his separatist ideas in those Spaniards living in North Africa.

Pepillo asked him, "Do you really believe that separating your region from the Iberian Peninsula is as easy as slicing yourself a slab of cod? Just try it and see how you take it off the map. Do you believe that because you have a strategic region with smelters and a steel industry you will be able to pay for education, health services, public works, justice, etc.? You Basques are all crazy." Galicians, Valencians, Andalusians all joined in the discussion. It turned into a shouting match.

A while later I fell ill. I lost all the strength in my knees and my nervous system was shot. Dr. Galván told me to take care of myself and ordered me to take it easy and rest, and, above all, not to think so much. He didn't know what he was asking of me. As time went by, I returned to the same agitated life I had always led, the life of all refugees with their groups or communities. And work. The customs agent became a metalworker. Another learned arc welding. A bureaucrat from one of the ministries had a small shop with a forge. He bought scrap aluminum and made magnificent spoons and forks. A man named Alberola, from Madrid, learned chemistry and manufactured, among other things, the homemade bleach sold under the brand name "Gloria." Another manufactured shoe polish.

In the end, we lost all confidence in the Americans. What was left of the words liberty and democracy? They were saying they would recognize the Franco government as legitimate. That would be the final blow to our struggle. The only ones left would be those of us who had the strongest convictions. The others would return home, little by little.

The Boat

Together with Juan Martínez Andújar, I bought a sardine trawler. It was abandoned in the Port and, with great tenacity, we made it new again. We embarked with some refugees who had to adapt to a new life, among them an aviation mechanic named Pedro Obispado, who was in charge of the boat's motor. Our "Mediouna" left the Port of Safi on March 3, 1944, at eleven o'clock at night, on an almost completely calm sea.[25] Some fifteen miles from the Port, we had arrived at the fishing ground. It was almost dawn. We set up a portable stove on deck to make breakfast and began to boil water in our coffee pot. It was March, the windy month. Ours was the only boat that had put out from the Port of Safi. We were feeding the trawl lines over the railing. Every few hundred meters along the line there was a cork slab with a bamboo pole on which we had raised a flag with the letter M. Eventually there were twenty flags floating along the line. A strong wind came up from the west and, with the first gusts, a wave came over the boat's

---

[25] In Miguel Domínguez Soler's manuscript, the date for this adventure is March 3, 1945. However, since he will later speak of the favorable war news as the Allies re-conquered more and more territory, I assume this to be an error.

deck, washing the portable stove and coffee pot overboard. A few minutes later, a larger wave carried off the only barrel of drinking water we had. It sank into the sea.

Our fishing master was a Moroccan, the old Rais Ouiga, who advised me to abandon the fishing ground immediately. Our motorman, who was now seasick, could not get the motor started and the boat was being pushed by the waves toward some cliffs. With a seventy meter line we carried on board, we dropped anchor. Once it set, the boat swung its bow westward. Everyone went below deck and I took up my post at the tiller to keep the boat from being broadsided by a wave. The swells grew ever larger and the slabs of cork with their flags disappeared. Our first ill-fated night at sea came upon us with the sky full of stars and the wind whistling through our mast and rigging. Some waves surged over our port side. This Calvary, without food or water, lasted three days and nights. On the third day, the wind relented and the flags suddenly appeared on the sea's surface. Pedro Obispado finally managed to start the motor and we were filled with rejoicing.

"All hands on deck," ordered Rais, the old Moroccan fishing master.

I passed my hands over my forehead and found salt crystals embedded in the skin. The crew began to haul in the trawl lines and toss into the hold the huge rays and dogfish that had eaten our catch. We set a course for Safi and arrived at four in the afternoon.

Many people had spread the word that we had sunk, because the Port's boats are not supposed to be out more than twenty-four hours. Antonio Campos, from Madrid, swore he would never again set foot on a boat as long as he lived. A useless oath. Our adventure is the way life goes at sea. Later, with an elbow on the bar and a glass of good wine, it was all forgotten.

The boat continued fishing. At least it provided food for the crew, which became proficient enough to carry on without me. Once I could remain ashore, I got busy setting up a fish meal factory, which I would soon have up and running. For me, nighttime was like a bad dream bringing memories of all that had happened. Everything was going well, but I was dissatisfied. I wanted to move on.

In Agadir

I was more than three hundred kilometers further south, near the Bou Irden fishing operation, twenty kilometers north of Agadir. I was enjoying the adventure. At night, my house overlooking the sea was surrounded by jackals. At times, even hyenas could be heard, neighing like colts. I had decided to come this far, to a place where no one knew me. I owed nothing to anybody. The lads back in Safi were earning a living with the boat. Some two hundred Spaniards were working the Bou Irden fishing operation, almost all of them from the area around Málaga. Since there was no drinking water here, the custom was to go fetch it from a spring that surged from among the rocks located a short distance away. At sunset, all the women would put a jug on their head and, either alone or in a group, walk the five hundred meters between the cannery and the spring. And it was precisely as the sun went down that the jackals would begin their hungry howling. They came in packs to the factory, where they could always find fish heads and entrails.

One evening, the women returned terrified and shrieking. They had seen an enormous panther roaring beside the spring. The inhabitants of the fishing operation had told us that, a few years before, a woman had left the cannery grounds carrying a jug on her head and leading her five-year-old daughter by the hand. When, two or three hours later, the woman had not returned, her husband and some of his neighbors went looking for her. Night had fallen. By the light of an oil lamp, they searched the area around the spring and found the poor woman dead. The panther had eaten her innards. They kept searching, but the little girl was never found. This tragedy belonged to the past and was all but forgotten. Every day at nightfall, the women kept going to the spring and had never again spoken of the terrible panther until the evening it reappeared.

Three days later, at four in the afternoon, Iziki the peddler was riding his burro through a dense grove of Argán trees on his way to the cannery. Suddenly, the burro pricked up its pointy ears and lowered its head, throwing Iziki to the ground and setting off in a desperate attempt to escape. Like a bolt of lightning, the terrible panther pounced from one of the tree limbs and, a few meters later, had his fangs in the neck of the burro, which fell to the ground, its legs kicking the air. Iziki, terrified, fled through the thicket in the direction of the cannery, where he arrived gasping and speechless. The men brought him a glass of water and, finally, he was able to tell us what had happened. The workers immediately left their posts and headed out to confront the feline. Some were armed with machetes and enormous tuna knives, and others with iron bars. When they arrived, the beast had already emptied the victim of all its internal organs. Two days later, the French authorities in Tamanar called on all the Europeans living in the region to join in a large hunting party which would beat the area and capture the feline.

I had a 1937 Chevrolet pickup with cast iron pistons, an electric fuel pump, and a cab for two people. There was enough room in the cargo box for four more people. The captain who commanded the region gave me a musket from the Brescia arms factory and three bullets. He warned me not to give the weapon to any of the Arabs. The forest rose from the beach to an elevation of some fifty meters and extended some seventy kilometers. The group had the mission of advancing eastward. More than forty men on horseback followed us, and there were mules to carry our provisions. Chandoul, who had been an army sergeant and fought the Germans under the French flag, rode with me in the cab. He kept eyeing my musket like someone coveting a toy. A firearm in his hands was a source of great joy to him. For me, it was an annoyance the way the bolt kept jabbing me in the back. There were four workers from the factory in the cargo box. They were armed with iron pipes. We drove slowly so we could spot the animal if it was up in one of those dense trees. It is often impossible to see one of those felines until you are right below it, because its fur blends in with the leaves. I had come prepared. I had with me a sack with several cans of sardines, bread, a banana, and a bottle of wine. Each of the others had rations for twenty-four hours. We encountered large beasts with enormous horns resembling those of mountain goats, gazelles that bolted away in terror, an occasional foul-smelling hyena, and dozens of wild boars. Just before sunset we arrived at the edge of a ravine. A bugle signaled for us to make camp.

We got out of the vehicle. I grabbed my sack, cut open my bread, and filled it with sardines. I began to eat, washing down my meal with a tasty wine. There was a boy who was a porter from the Inmuser des Ida u Tanan school. Chandoul sent him out to gather firewood so we could boil water for tea. A coffee pot and a jerrycan full of water were unloaded from the mules. The only topic of discussion was the five thousand franc bonus the captain had offered for whoever handed over the panther's skin. With an incentive like that, there were those who saw panthers everywhere. Two all-terrain vehicles belonging to the Forest Guards arrived and joined us. The guards were armed with rifles. Dr. Pacud also arrived. None of the members of the different groups had seen anything out of the ordinary. The sun had gone down and night was setting in on that highland in the center of the forest.

Hamed, the school porter, returned in a state of alarm, telling Chandoul, "I just now saw something like an enormous cat entering a cave over there down the mountain. Maybe it is the panther."

Chandoul smiled and told him, "Alright. Let's have a glass of tea and then we will go have a look."

"No," Hamed replied, "don't you see it is getting dark? Later, we will be unable to catch him."

Having said that, he began running down the mountainside, with a stick in his right hand and a lantern in his left.

"Chandoul, get up!" I said. "We can't let him go out alone."

"I know it isn't the panther."

"But what if it is?"

We too ran down the mountainside. Chandoul asked for my musket and a bullet. He kissed the firearm, opened the bolt and, within a second, loaded the bullet with extraordinary facility. We were a few meters away when Hamed took up his place in front of the grotto. He lit the lamp and everything happened in a flash. There was a roar. Hamed ran but, in one leap, the animal had him by the right leg. Then there was a heart-rending scream and Chandoul's well-aimed shot that passed through the left ear of the monster, which fell heavily on top of Hamed. We saw that he was bleeding profusely. Chandoul handed me the musket and thanked me. "The musket is yours, but the panther is mine," he said.

Drawn by the gunshot, dozens of people were coming down the mountain. Many of them congratulated me because they thought I had been the one who fired the shot. Hamed was soon being treated by Dr. Pacud, who was trying to close a deep gash about eight centimeters long in the back of his right thigh. A group of men carried him on their shoulders to the mountaintop and, from there, the doctor transported him to the Agadir hospital.

Eight men with four poles hoisted the panther and carried him to one of the forest guards' vehicles, where Chandoul took a seat and argued heatedly with the French, who asked me for my identity card and wrote my name in their service records, but I protested that the bonus should be given to Chandoul. Since the forest was now completely dark, the order went out that no one was to leave until dawn. Everyone gathered around the bonfires while hundreds of hungry jackals howled. The following day, with the workers back at the factory and the ships out fishing, everyone treated me with respect and was extraordinarily courteous to the "fugitives," as they called us Spaniards.

It was at about this time that I met a friend of Monsieur Mallein who came to visit the cannery. He proposed that I take charge of an important factory he planned to open in Agadir. I accepted at once. In that city, I would have all the conveniences required for modern life. The Bou Irden cannery provided a good living, but it was located in an uninhabited area at the foot of the Atlas Mountains where there was neither running water nor electricity.

"Here you have two acres of terrain covered with spiny cactus. Gather a team to clear it, and draw up a list of all the materials you need to process as much as thirty thousand kilos of fish per day. We already have our first boat to fish for the factory. It is named 'Chanterelle.' Make sure it has all the nets it needs," he told me.

I was down at the entrance to the Port, when I saw a fine sardine boat come in. Its registration number began with the letter H for Huelva. "This could be people from Ayamonte," I said to myself. Sure enough, it was the "Pepe." I had already been informed by people who worked these fishing grounds that in the southeastern region of the Iberian Peninsula, the main source of wealth, sardines, had completely disappeared. The boats there had to load up with salt and come down here to fish, salting their catch so it wouldn't spoil on the return trip. I waited a few minutes while the boat tied up to the pier and, with my heart pounding in anticipation, went over to make contact with the crew.

I approached the boat. Some of the men saw me, but no one recognized me. Finally, I greeted them with a "Good evening to all," and they identified me at once. What a happy moment! I felt like I was home again. There were embraces and relentless questions. I told them I would come for them that night and we would have supper together in my house. It would give me the illusion that I was in my native land.

I climbed the hill to my house, which was located on a corner of the terrain where the factory was being built. Several people, men and women, set to work preparing a meat and potato stew. I had to make three trips with my pickup in order to transport the whole crew. "What we have been through, we will never forget until the day we die," they told me. For me, it was a day of celebration. We ate and drank great quantities of African wine while talking endlessly of my beloved Andalusia. Many of these men had been prisoners in the jail or in the Creoli Cinema.

There was a moment of frightful silence. Marcelo, the eldest son of 'El Marcelo,' was talking. In his seaman's language, he described the bitterest moments of his life. "There are many nights," he said, "when I am awake, but dreaming a cruel nightmare. My heart jumps and it seems as if it wants to pop out through my mouth. What we have seen cannot be forgotten as long as we live. I see the tragic scene of the 'massacres.' Midnight. The silence of the cells. The noise of the truck that stops at the door to the jail. Someone murmurs, 'Here they are.' A few seconds. The door bolt groans as it is slid open. Everyone's hair stands on end. Everyone sits up, like automatons, so they can hear better. Heartbeats accelerate. There are some whose teeth chatter like castanets. Now the cell door opens. The corridor is full of Falangists. One of them takes out a list, the fateful list. The first name is read. A man is condemned to death. Everyone looks at him for the last time. There are those who clench their teeth until they make a grinding sound in their mouth. 'Out,' orders a voice from the corridor. And the condemned man goes out, without strength, and without knowing how many hours of life he has left. Then the second name on the list. And so on, until the number reaches twenty-four. Panic. Terror. One cries in a silence filled with fear and rage. Now they are all in the truck and the door closes. One hears the truck depart. We have a knot in our throats. Deep sighs are exhaled, and the sound of the truck's gears fills us momentarily with happiness. We are safe for now. One more day of life. Maybe tomorrow night it will be my turn."

Marcelo had shriveled our hearts with his terrifying tale of the "massacres." It is I who call out words of encouragement, "Let's drink and sing! The storm has passed. Let's make sure the next one doesn't catch us unprepared." The supper lasted until two-thirty in the morning while we talked about all that had happened during these years of separation. I made three more trips to the Port, returning the crew to their boat, because the following day they had to work. How they will talk of me when they get back to the town!

The Little Moorish Girl

Abouch, the little Moorish girl who used to take care of my house and wash my clothes, has arrived. She came with her whole family, which has traveled to Agadir in search of work. I have taken her in with great fondness because, in truth, I was very much in need of her. A bachelor's house is a messy house, with dirty clothes strewn here and there, and with the sink full of unwashed plates and spoons. I was so very busy, I had no time to tend to the house. The girl's older brother, who had been the chauffer of Colonel Justinard of the French resistance in Rabat, also came to my house. We were talking a long time. The whole family found work, one as a truck driver transporting rocks to build the factory, and all the others as construction workers.

The great problem that loomed as the factory neared completion was the lack of a feminine workforce. The region, populated by Berbers, consisted of fairly well-off families. Almost every family had a male relative with an established business somewhere, from Tangiers and Melilla to the Sahara. The women and children stayed in the *duares*, as they called their villages, caring for the livestock. For a sardine factory, the number of women available for the canning operation is of utmost importance. For that reason, I gave orders to first construct twenty rooms in a row, each room containing four cots and divided into two blocks. In the area between the blocks, there would be two water faucets and two bathrooms. There remained the task of recruiting these nearly one hundred women. The most skilled workers, who were Spanish speaking, came from Ifni. Others had arrived from the Spanish Sahara, a waterless area of great thirst where the only food was goat or camel milk.

I could also count on Chinguiti, a young man who came all the way from the Mauritanian border and was the most talented of my employees for running errands or handling phone calls when I wasn't there. One fine day, when work was done, he suggested I send him with the truck to Semara and Villa Cisneros. He would take charge of bringing me one hundred women or more from that region of poverty and hunger. For centuries, it had been Morocco, with its fishing, phosphate, cattle, and industrial wealth, which alleviated the demographic problem of that large territory patrolled by Spanish legionnaires. Since Morocco had established strict border controls to avoid the entry of products from the Canary Islands, I wrote a letter to the gentleman who was in charge of the border between the two regions, asking him to give free passage to the personnel assigned to my factory, which would be beneficial to the Spaniards in charge of those groups of impoverished nomads.

Fifteen days after they left, Chinguiti and his driver Mohaite returned with forty women in the truck. That same day, they left again to pick up forty more women who were still there waiting. A team from Casablanca was putting a roof on the factory and installing two boilers, sterilizers, cookers, tables, vats for the cooking oils, and tanks for the fuels.

Once my whereabouts were known, my compatriots, the sardine fishermen, show up almost every day to see me, but I have little time to receive them as they deserve. So 'Gorito,' my cousin Diego González, 'Little Mackerel' from Isla Cristina, and so many other friends would spend a few hours with me in the hope that I could return to Spain after its liberation. The war news was more favorable for the Allies with each passing day. Each triumph, each reconquest of territory where the enemy suffered a defeat was a cause for celebration or, even more, a reason to hope for a speedy return to my homeland.

Production

When the first five thousand kilograms of sardines arrived at the factory, it turned out to be tedious work to teach these inexperienced employees how to remove the heads, cut off the tails, and pack the sardines into cans; or to teach the boiler operators to maintain pressure at six kilos; and then to show Salah, my little Moorish girl's brother, how to sterilize cans in the autoclaves; or to teach the youngest brother, Larbi, how to cook fish in the huge iron ovens. Work that should have taken a couple of hours has cost me six hours nonstop. Once these five thousand kilos were finished, and with one hour of rest, the "Chanterelle" has caught ten thousand kilograms more, and the truck has transported them from the Port to the factory in two trips. Once more, we begin the tasks of washing, gutting, removing heads and tails, brining, and canning. But with each load, we get faster. A second truck begins gathering little girls between fourteen and twenty years old from the area around Agadir who, like all Berbers, are very fond of earning money.

In this way, I put together a team of specialists, almost all of them the relatives of the little Moorish girl who lived in my house. I had been entirely on my own, but now I was gathering a tight-knit family around me, a family that collaborated with me and for whom I provided all the facilities they required. The results could not have turned out better. Monsieur Mallein and his friend phoned to congratulate me for getting the factory up and running, and to wish me continued success with my endeavor. The news spread throughout the Sahara that there was a fortune to be made in Agadir, and groups began arriving on foot. Whole families come with their goats and camels. Soon a settlement with more than five thousand inhabitants has established itself behind the factory. They lay squares of stone and cover them with roofs made of goat and camel skins, creating *jaimas*, the tents used by desert nomads. The men work on the construction of the factories which, following my example, begin to multiply, providing employment for the women but causing me to lose a good deal of time in consultations with the many novice industrialists.

Manuel Flores Rodríguez, the former mayor of Ayamonte, and Miguel Gómez Barranco each established their own separate factory. Flores had to be hospitalized when he contracted a serious throat ailment. The last thing any of us expected came to pass and he spent six cruel months in a special room at the Agadir Hospital. In a last-ditch effort to save him, a tracheotomy was performed and he died at six o'clock in the morning, far from the affection of his children. All of us refugees, accompanied by French friends, went to his burial. One by one, we are disappearing the same way, leaving our remains in foreign soil.

Miguel Gómez Barranco did not like Agadir. The work was intense and Miguel missed his everyday friends and, above all, the daily gatherings in some café. One fine day, he packed up and went to live in the great metropolis of Casablanca, but not for long. A short while later, just like Flores, he would sigh his last breath, far from his children and family.

Cada Oveja con su Pareja[26]

It was a saying I tried not to take seriously. Since I met her in Safi, my little Moorish girl and I maintained the most intimate amorous relations. She was my maid, my woman, and my collaborator in the factory. She had learned to speak Spanish before I mastered Arabic. She knew I had a fiancée and that as long as my fiancée lived, we could not be married, but for Abouch Spain was far away and there was a barrier of enormous obstacles that prevented me from returning to my homeland. I was oblivious to racial differences. When young, one confronts the most adverse circumstances without taking into account the consequences. She had been born under the green flag of Islam, a traditional religion deeply rooted in the family and, for them, it was an offense for a daughter to fall in love, not to mention form a couple, with a *sarani*, a foreigner.

Neither she nor I made a secret of our relationship. She used to cling to my arm when we went out to eat or watch a movie. One day, when we didn't have to work, we were in a restaurant and a zealous Muslim who saw the

---
26 A saying in rhyme which means, "Every sheep with its mate."

difference between her wheat-colored skin and mine, denounced her. They scorned us Europeans and saw it as abnormal that a Moroccan girl would be seen in public with a foreigner. The kindest thing they would call her in the street was "renegade." More than once, I had to resort to fisticuffs with one of these fanatics. They have the right to sleep with any European girl they meet, especially if she is a Scandinavian who, when feeling the need for a man, comes looking for Muslims. And these men stroll about with those blue-eyed blondes as if they had made a triumphal conquest. They have the right to enjoy European girls, but beware of touching one of the local girls. According to the Muslim religion, there are terrible punishments for those girls. Abouch and I laughed at all religions. Our religion was our love, our destiny, our work. To create, to transform each day, to make life easier and more perfect.

Each of her brothers was a technician by now. I had fewer worries and, at home, one of Abouch's sisters-in-law had a place to live and was in charge of the kitchen and the housekeeping.

"On my fateful road someone sows sorrows for me to reap," the poet said. One day, I received the sad news of my fiancée's death in Barcelona and knew exactly what to do. I went to see the French mayor of Agadir, Monsieur Villar, and presented our birth certificates and an authorization from Abouch's eldest brother, giving his consent to our marriage.

Twenty days later, she put on her suit with its "Prince of Wales" jacket and we went to the city hall. Monsieur Pierre Wacquez and his wife Paulette were there to serve as witnesses. The ceremony was simple and short. Cakes and bottles of champagne sealed the legalization of our marriage, after which we were given the necessary documentation to justify our union before the entire world.

Another five years passed. Encounters with men from my home town were an almost daily event. Every day, boats from Ayamonte put into port and the crew would bring me news from the town and tell me of its suffering under the Franco dictatorship.

The factory's production increased day by day, but I was being exploited. The board of directors shared the profits among themselves and with the bank, without considering my contribution. I gave them twenty-four hours notice. Either they pay me a greater share, or I would leave immediately. When my deadline expired, I notified Abouch's family so they could continue at their posts, because I had better opportunities elsewhere. With great sorrow, my wife and I departed that night for Casablanca.

Casablanca

Everything had been prepared for me beforehand. My friends from "refugeeland" and the members of the Moroccan League for Human Rights welcomed me with open arms. They had always thought I would never return to this great city. The García Lorca Circle and the Hispano-Portuguese Club were here, as well as a worthy number of organizations that worked for the re-conquest of Spain. I was soon elected to a place on the League's national committee and was invited to give the opening speech at a rally against the Spanish dictatorship in the Rif Cinema. With a packed house and even more people gathered in the street, I could satisfy my need to express myself freely and proclaim, with all the strength my lungs would allow, my total rejection of the cruel and archaic regime that had condemned us to exile. That meeting was an international success.

The following day, we were received by General Dris Ben Aomar, the governor of Casablanca, who interrogated us about the purpose of the Moroccan League for Human Rights and our attitude toward the Moroccan government. Our representative, Abdelkader Sadiki, explained the mission of the Universal Declaration of Human Rights passed on December 10, 1948, by the General Assembly of the United Nations. After the interview, the general saluted us cordially, and we left satisfied.

Since I was collaborating with Central and South American newspapers, I was given a press pass as the exclusive North African correspondent for the Mexican periodical *Panorama*. I have time to spare, and sort through my letters from Rafael Gómez Casado, who suffered through the siege of Madrid. In one of his letters to me, he writes, "When the air raid sirens went off, we would have to descend in complete darkness from the fifth floor to the basement, where the temporary air raid refuge was located. Imagine the chaos that reigned when the people living in the building all had to rush down the stairways at the same time. Men, women, children, and the elderly, weeping and crying out in terror, one of them falling over here, another falling over there. The darkness would make the scene even more pathetic. Meanwhile, the droning of motors could be heard as the German bombers we used to call *Pavas* approached, and then the whistling of the bombs as they fell and, not far off, the sound of explosions. We would feel a great trembling of the earth and feel comforted because we were still alive. These unpleasant visits could come in the morning, in the afternoon, or at night. Later, we would hear the news of the deaths caused by the bombardment. And on top of that, there was the scarcity. Often, our breakfast was a tomato with a little salt." These letters fill me with an enormous sorrow. I ask myself what had become of all those who offered their lives with so much love and affection for the Republic. Because the Republic was the true Spain.

One of his other letters, the one that made the deepest impression on me, was the one in which he announced the execution of Don Blas Infante Pérez, the notary who lived on Isla Cristina. It took place on the tenth day of that bloody August, the month when I was supposed to have fallen, and it affected me deeply because I was Blas Infante's disciple, perhaps the only one. Working as a scribe in the Ayamonte notary's office, I had the good fortune to form a friendship with Don Blas. At the time, he was well-known in the region's intellectual circles and, thanks to his facile pen, he was able to make a name for himself with his articles in the national press. I was publishing my poor efforts in a local weekly, *La Higuerita* [The Little Fig Tree]. We took to each other at once and, ideologically, I adopted his concept of Andalusianism in spite of his friendship with the anarchists of the CNT. What marvelous memories! I used to take my ever-present bicycle and ride the thirty-two kilometers from Ayamonte to Isla Cristina and back, filled with enthusiasm and eager to hear his wise words that were of such benefit to me.

Isla Cristina was a real island that its inhabitants had created by gouging up the sea's womb in revenge for the victims which that sea had so often made of the area's brave fishermen. The island consisted of dredged sand and, once in place, it grew higher each year, centimeter by centimeter, as the wind brought more sand. For that reason, one had to descend a few large steps in order to enter Don Blas's notary office. I never understood why, as a man from the interior, Don Blas ended up here, without relatives, as if an exile, living at the edge of the sea and putting up with the roar of the waves through nights of savage storms. Across from his house was the Isleño Casino and, every Saturday afternoon, I would find myself there with him, drinking coffee, while his German shepherd "Trotsky" slept at his feet.

The Factory

My friends and comrades kept me as busy as did my job at a factory dedicated exclusively to the canning of tuna. Those enormous tunas, some weighing almost five hundred kilograms, came from Kenitra or Larache. They had to be chopped up and canned as quickly as possible. It took hours, and sometimes I would see the dawn of a new day before falling exhausted into bed. And so the days passed, and the months and years, until that day the Spanish Constitution was proclaimed and Don Juan Carlos was crowned king of Spain.

Homecoming

It was September 16, 1983. Filled with delight, I was explaining all the sights to my wife. I had been warned to be careful in Seville, where there were many muggers. My wife had a handbag on her lap with the documents for the car, our passports, our identification cards, and all the papers we possessed. It was about three in the afternoon and the heat was oppressive as I braked for a red light on the Avenida de la Raza. Suddenly, with feline swiftness, one of two individuals who were on a motorcycle opened the right door of the car and snatched the bag from my wife's lap. She was startled. By the time I got out of the car it was too late. A businessman shouted from the sidewalk, "For shame!"

In this way I was welcomed home to my Spain. This Spain of ours.

About the Translator

Richard Barker was born September 11, 1945, the year Fascism was defeated everywhere in Europe except Spain. There it would last another thirty years. On Richard's twenty-eighth birthday, General Augusto Pinochet overthrew the democratically elected president of Chile, Salvador Allende, and consolidated his power with a bloody repression. And we all remember what happened on Richard's fifty-sixth birthday. He has sometimes wondered if the day he was born the stars were aligned in such a way that he was fated to spend a good deal of his life studying repression, terrorism, and Fascism in its Hispanic variety, which is a peculiar combination of military authoritarianism and ultraconservative Catholicism reminiscent of the Inquisition.

Richard lived in Spain during the 1965/66 academic year, studying at the University of Madrid. The country was still ruled by General Francisco Franco, and Richard saw subtle indications of the lasting effects of the civil war that had brought Franco to power. The trolley cars had seats with signs that said *Reservado para caballeros mutilados de la guerra* [Reserved for gentlemen mutilated in the war], and no one spoke publicly of politics unless they agreed with the versions available in the nation's three newspapers: *Ya* (Catholic), *Arriba* (Fascist), and *Abc* (pro-Franco).

As elsewhere in the world in the mid-sixties, there was unrest. One sunny spring day, Richard was returning from class on his Vespa and found himself in the middle of a pitched battle between students wielding Mao signs and throwing Molotov cocktails, and police firing rubber bullets from automatic weapons. In comparison to the University of Madrid, whatever happened that year at Berkeley or Columbia would seem like a friendly game of tag. The next day there was nothing in Spain's newspapers about what had occurred. Not one word.

Richard's trusty Vespa also took him on adventures to many places in Spain and Portugal. One of them was Cuelgamuros, where Franco had built a mausoleum for himself and for tens of thousands of *Caídos por dios y la patria* [the Fallen for God and the Fatherland]. The basilica is hollowed out of a mountain and the entrance is in the monumental style of the Nazi architect Albert Speer, but on the mountain top there is an enormous cross instead of a swastika. The construction took twenty years, from 1939 to 1959, and was carried out, as Richard learned later, by political prisoners in a program called *Redención de Penas por el Trabajo* [Redemption of Sentences through Labor].

The next time Richard went to Spain, it was to teach English at the University of Seville during the 1979/80 academic year. He has a wonderful souvenir from that stay, his wife Carmen. Not only has she given him thirty years of marital bliss, she also introduced him to the people of her home town, Castilleja del Campo (pop. 600). They are the subject of his life work, an oral history of the town during the Republic, the civil war, and the Franco years: *El largo trauma de un pueblo andaluz: República, represión, guerra, posguerra* (Castilleja del Campo: Ayuntamiento, 2007). It was during his research for that book that he encountered Miguel Domínguez Soler's Memoir.

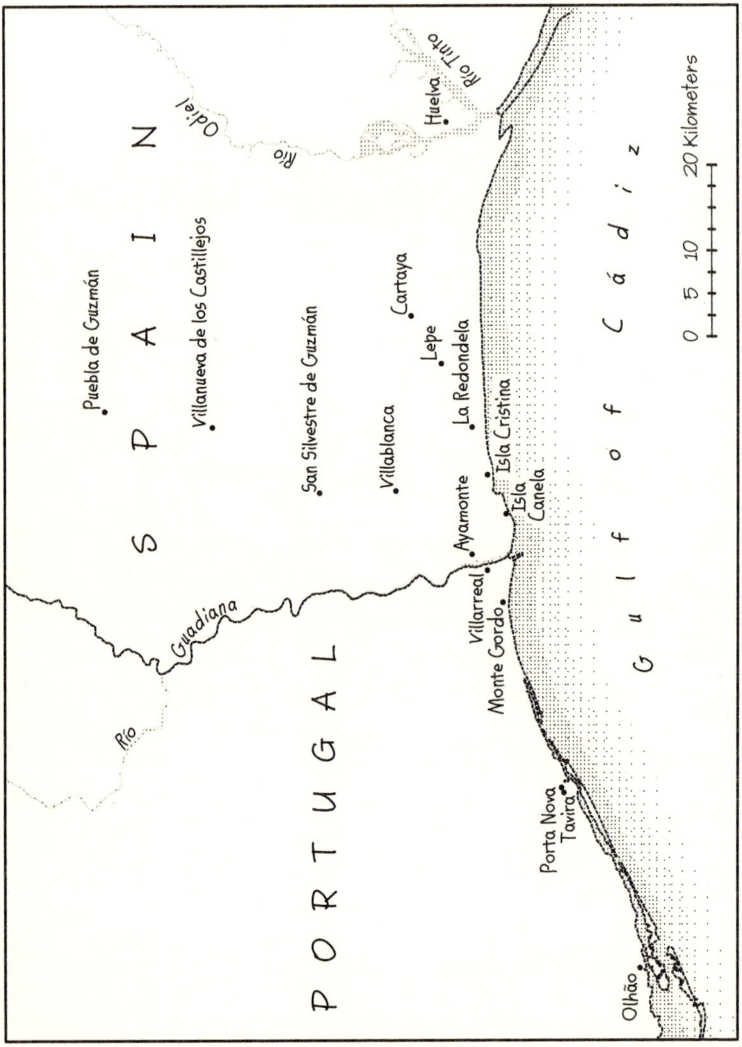

SPAIN
PORTUGAL
Gulf of Cádiz
Puebla de Guzmán
Villanueva de los Castillejos
San Silvestre de Guzmán
Villablanca
Cartaya
Lepe
La Redondela
Isla Cristina
Isla Canela
Ayamonte
Villarreal
Monte Gordo
Porta Nova
Tavira
Olhão
Huelva
Río Tinto
Río Odiel
Guadiana
Río
0 5 10 20 Kilometers

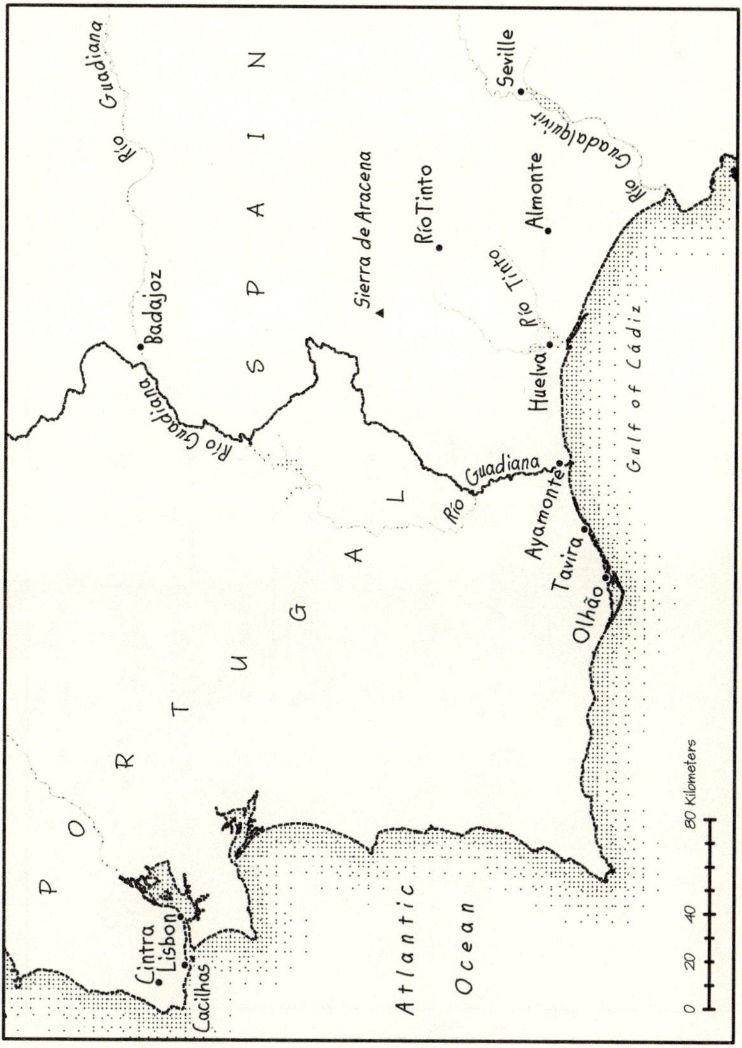
P O R T U G A L
S P A I N
Río Guadiana
Badajoz
Río Guadiana
Sierra de Aracena
Río Tinto
Río Tinto
Almonte
Seville
Río Guadalquivir
Huelva
Río Guadiana
Ayamonte
Tavira
Olhão
Gulf of Cádiz
Cintra
Lisbon
Cacilhas
Atlantic Ocean
0 20 40 80 Kilometers

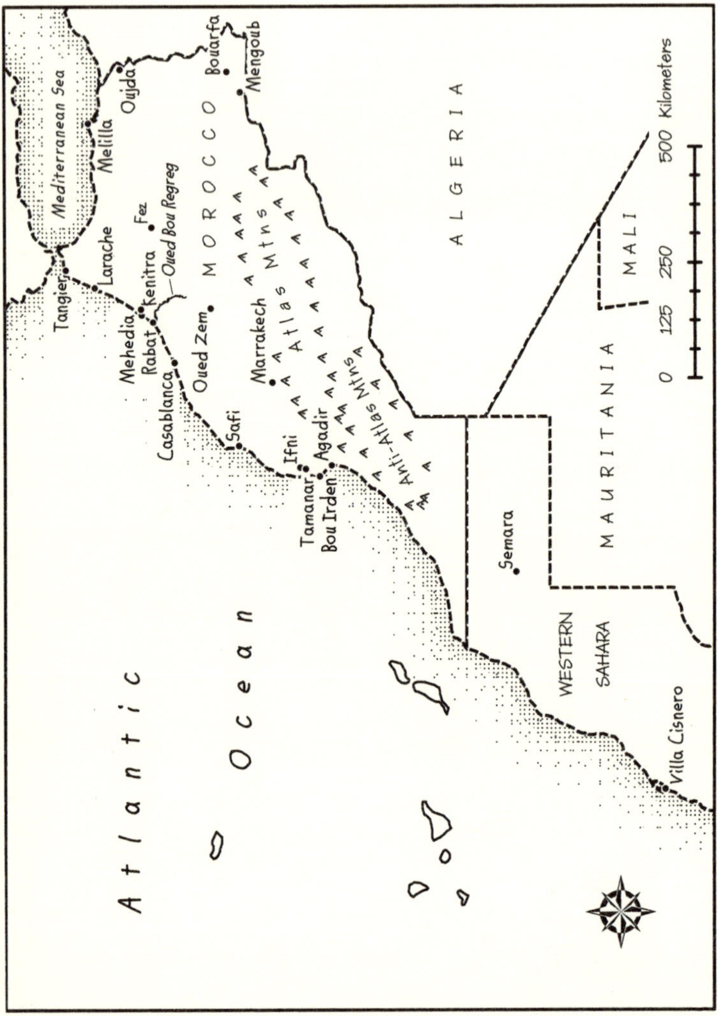
Atlantic
Ocean
Mediterranean Sea
Tangier
Larache
Melilla
Oujda
Mehedia
Kenitra
Rabat
Oued Bou Regreg
Fez
Casablanca
Oued Zem
M O R O C C O
Bouarfa
Mengoub
Safi
Marrakech
Atlas Mtns
Ifni
Agadir
Tamanar
Bou Irden
Anti-Atlas Mtns
A L G E R I A
M A L I
M A U R I T A N I A
Semara
WESTERN
SAHARA
Villa Cisnero
0
125
250
500
Kilometers

235

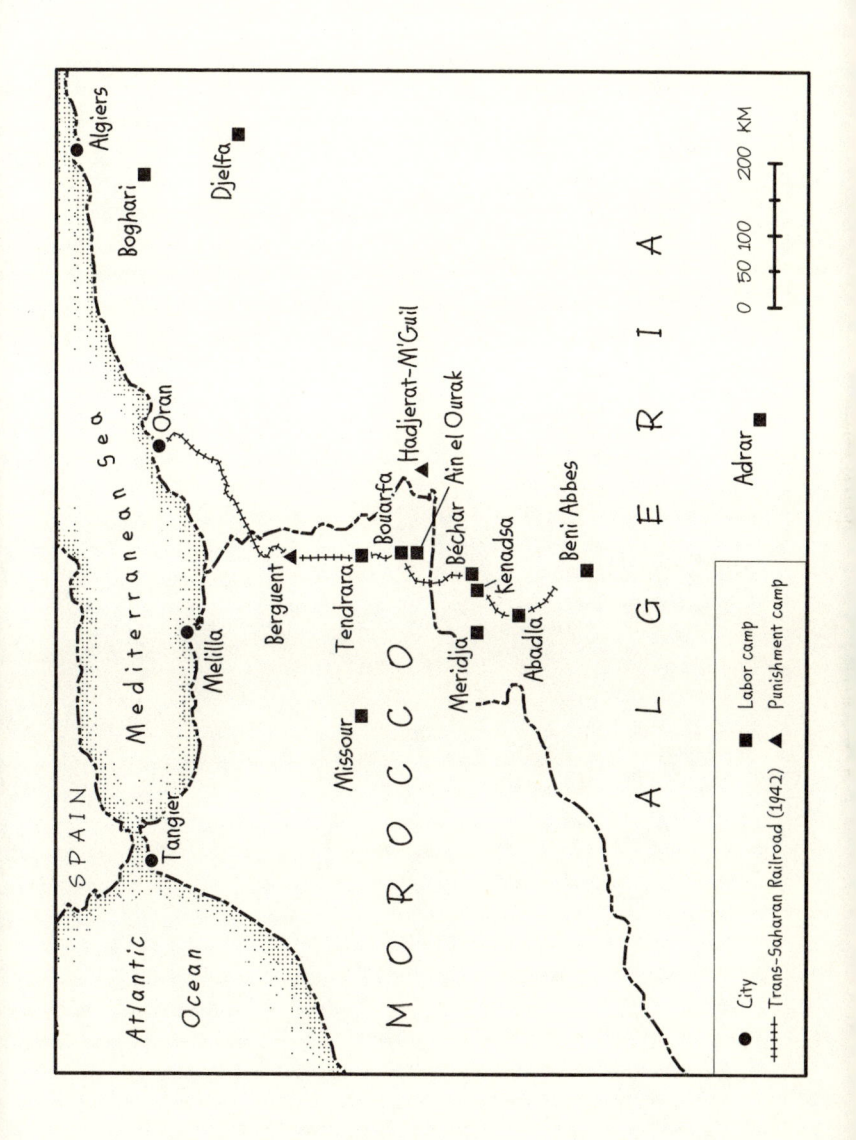

Cornerstone Press '09 Team

CEO	Dan Dieterich
President	Kyle Bernander
Corporate Secretary	Jeremy Larson
Editor-in-Chief	Lauren Shimulunas
Managing Editor	Andrew Stepan
Marketing Manager	Melinda McCord
Sales Manager	Amy VanMeter
Advertising Manager	Katelynn Paape
Substance Editor	Lee Wickman
-Associates	Eric Rueth
	Allison Herr
	Tanner Hoffman
	John Leonhardt
Copyeditor	Amanda Waddington
-Associates	Philecia Pribnow
	Emily Fish
	Ty Natzke
Publicity Director	Erin Mueller
Fulfillment Manager	Ty Natzke
Co-Production Managers	Kacie Otto
	Tracy Berg
Business Manager	Krystle Fandrey
Designer	Scott Gerstl
Webmaster	Falan Shulfer

Cornerstone Press '10 Team

CEO — Per Henningsgaard
President — Mike Gorham
Corporate Secretary — Claire Hogan
Editor-in-Chief — Aaron Osowski

Managing Editor — James Ziech

Marketing Manager — Andrew Tully
-Associate — Leah Wierzba

Sales Manager — Andrea Meister
Advertising Manager — Thea Tracanna

Substance Editor — Rachel Werner
-Associates — Abby Hoeft
Keri Kobussen
Martin Smith

Copyeditor — Rebecca Adams
-Associates — Catherine Binkowski
Brianna McKichan

Publicity Director — Patrick J. Sheehan
Fulfillment Manager — Joelle Verhagen

Production Manager — Laura May Spencer
-Associate — Laura Hartle

Business Manager — Jenna Diedrich

Designer — Laura Gang
-Associates — Ben Cisewski
Nichole Marik

Webmaster — Zach Schuett